# Reading, Writing, and Gender

## Instructional Strategies and Classroom Activities that Work for Girls and Boys

Gail Lynn Goldberg

Barbara Sherr Roswell

EYE ON EDUCATION

6 DEPOT WAY WEST, SUITE 106

LARCHMONT, NY 10538

(914) 833–0551

(914) 833–0761 fax

www.eyeoneducation.com

**Library of Congress Cataloging-in-Publication Data**

Goldberg, Gail Lynn, 1950-
    Reading, writing, and gender : instructional strategies and classroom activities that work for girls and boys / Gail Lynn Goldberg, Barbara Sherr Roswell.
        p. cm.
        Includes bibliographical references.
    ISBN 1-930556-23-3
    1. Language arts. 2. Children--Books and reading. 3. Sex differences in education. I. Roswell, Barbara Sherr, 1959- II. Title.
    LB 1576 .G68 2002
    372.6--dc21

                                                                        2001040359

10 9 8 7 6 5 4

Editorial and production services provided by
Richard H. Adin Freelance Editorial Services
52 Oakwood Blvd., Poughkeepsie, NY 12603-4112
(845-471-3566)

## *Also Available from* EYE ON EDUCATION

**Assessment Portfolios for Elementary Students**
Milwaukee Public Schools

**Buddies: Reading, Writing and Math Lessons**
Pia Hansen Powell

**Better Instruction Through Assessment:
What Your Students Are Trying to Tell You**
Leslie Walker Wilson

**Teaching, Learning, & Assessment:
The Reflective Classroom**
Arthur K. Ellis

**Open Ended Questions in Elementary Mathematics:
Instruction and Assessment**
Mary Kay Dyer and Christine Moynihan

**Technology Tools for Young Learners**
Leni von Blanckensee

**Developing Parent and Community
Understanding of Performance-Based Assessment**
Kathryn Alvestad

**A Collection of Performance Tasks & Rubrics:
Primary School Mathematics**
Charlotte Danielson and Pia Hansen Powell

**A Collection of Performance Tasks & Rubrics:
Upper Elementary School Mathematics**
Charlotte Danielson

**Mathematics the Write Way:
Activities for Every Elementary Classroom**
Marilyn Neil

# TABLE OF CONTENTS

# ABOUT THE AUTHORS

**Gail Lynn Goldberg** is an educational consultant who works with schools and school systems to improve instruction and classroom assessment. Prior to becoming a consultant four years ago, Gail worked for a decade as an assessment specialist with the Maryland State Department of Education (MSDE)—first directing the Maryland Writing Test (MWT), and then in a leadership role with the Maryland School Performance Assessment Program (MSPAP)—experiences that deepened her appreciation for the ways assessment can be a window into teaching and learning. Gail has her Ph.D. in English Literature from the Graduate Center, City University of New York, and taught writing, comparative arts, and literature before shifting her primary focus toward the impact of assessment on classroom practice.

**Barbara Sherr Roswell** teaches English, linguistics, and women's studies at Goucher College in Maryland, where she has also directed the writing program and the writing center. She holds a Masters in English Education from New York University and a Ph.D. from the University of Pennsylvania's Program in Reading, Writing and Literacy. Barbara serves as the Editor of *Reflections*, a journal devoted to community-based writing and service-learning pedagogy. Among her favorite courses to teach is a seminar in "Gender and Language."

Gail and Barbara first met when they joined the faculty at Goucher College. Their friendship and professional relationship have thrived for nearly twenty years, during which they have collaborated on many papers, presentations, and research projects in the areas of reading and writing assessment, performance-based instruction, and gender and literacy. Never far from their minds are their children—Gail's two grown sons and Barbara's two preteen sons and young daughter—whose literacy learning has been a constant source of insight and inspiration. To all of them—Ethan, Justin, Michael, David, and Naomi—this book is dedicated.

# ACKNOWLEDGMENTS

This book might never have become a reality were it not for the many teachers and instructional leaders with whom the topic of literacy and gender resonated so powerfully. Their curiosity about ways that boys and girls are "differently literate" and their deep commitment to helping all their students achieve drove both our investigation and our development of instructional strategies.

We are grateful to the many classroom teachers, resource teachers, instructional specialists and school and district leaders who were partners in inquiry and who were instrumental in implementing and refining many of the activities we describe in this book. We especially wish to acknowledge with appreciation: Timonium Elementary and Lutherville Elementary (Baltimore County, Maryland); Cecil Manor Elementary School, Gilpin Manor Elementary School, North East Elementary School, Elkton Middle School (Cecil County, Maryland); Dr. James Craik Elementary School, Gale-Bailey Elementary School, Daniel of St. Thomas Jenifer Elementary School, Mary H. Matula Elementary School and Mattawoman Middle School (Charles County, Maryland); and Benjamin Banneker Elementary School (St. Mary's County, Maryland).

In particular, we extend our thanks to the following individuals (listed alphabetically by affiliation) who read the manuscript with care or contributed specific resources: Lorna Leone, principal, Four Seasons Elementary School (Anne Arundel County Public Schools); Carol Brannach and Tina Martin, learning resource teachers, Robert Gerard, principal, Elkton Middle School, and Gary Richardson, instructional coordinator for staff development (Cecil County Public Schools); Nancy Healy, Title I helping teacher, Judy Gieger Gordon, Melanie Sweezy, and Lisa Wisniewski, resource teachers, Noel Miller, media specialist, and Susie Fowler, principal, Daniel of St. Thomas Jenifer Elementary School (Charles County Public Schools); JoAnn Fruchtman, The Children's Bookstore, Baltimore; Shauna Kelley and Sarajane Snyder, research assistants, Pam Scheff, assistant professor of English, and Susan Stocker, associate professor of philosophy, Goucher College; Ron Levitan, fourth grade teacher and Laura Schlitz, librarian, The Park School, Baltimore; and Todd Falk, System Source.

For years, our husbands Andrew Goldberg and Bob Roswell have welcomed our projects, which, like long-term guests, have taken over our dining room tables, stairways, and any spare room in our homes and our lives. Our thanks to them both for their patience and encouragement during all phases of this project.

# PREFACE

Either through experience or anecdote, you are likely to be familiar with the study in which participants were asked to "draw a scientist." For nearly half a century, the image created in response by boys and girls, men and women, has been overwhelmingly male. Even when this study was repeated within the last decade, 100% of the boys and 84% of the girls asked to "draw a scientist" were still drawing men (Sadker & Sadker, 1994, p. 123). These percentages remind us that gender stereotypes are slow to change and still prevail—not just when it comes to mathematics and science, but also when it comes to language and literacy.

To demonstrate, we ask you to picture a reader. Who do you see? Almost every adult we ask visualizes a woman. Next, reflect for a few moments on your mental image of a woman reading. What has she got in her hands? The hundreds of times we've asked this question, we're told, "a book," "a novel," "a romance," "a women's magazine." Now, picture a man reading. What has he got in his hands? This time, the responses are typically "a newspaper," "a manual," or "a magazine on sports or cars." In our personal worlds, as in our professional ones, men and women, boys and girls, are likely to be perceived as "differently literate." Although teachers, instructional leaders, parents, and students themselves clearly bring gendered assumptions, expectations, and behaviors to reading and writing, these have rarely been made explicit and have even less often been evaluated for the power to support or impede students' literacy learning.

Your having this book in hand suggests that you, like an increasing number of teachers and others interested in education, recognize that boys and girls do indeed often behave differently as readers and writers. For example, you may have noticed that girls gravitate towards literary selections whereas boys often prefer informational texts, or that girls tend to compose stories of relationships reflecting multiple perspectives whereas boys' stories typically are plot-driven and feature a single male protagonist. The ever-increasing frequency of testing and attention to accountability have highlighted that these are differences not just of preference but also of performance. On formal measures of achievement, like state and national assessments, girls consistently outperform boys in the areas of both reading and writing.

Although some people shrug their shoulders and attribute these differences to boys' slower maturation, greater activity level, or some more general notion that "boys will be boys" and can't be expected to sustain the same degree of interest or involvement in creating or interpreting text, we have learned otherwise. Differences in behaviors do indeed exist, but those in performance need not. Our challenge is to understand and honor the fact that whenever children are doing activities involving reading or writing, gender shapes, but should not limit, what they do.

By highlighting gender issues in this book, we have of necessity given less attention to individual differences and "exceptions to the rule," as well as to the many similarities that can be found between boys' and girls' literacy learning. We thus risk reinforcing some of the very stereotypes we wish to challenge. Yet we believe that the risk of ignoring differences is greater than the danger of discussing them, and no student is well served by ignoring possible obstacles to his or her learning.

In the pages that follow, we therefore first offer some general background in Part I about what research—our own as well as others'— tells us about boys and girls as readers and writers. We then draw upon this knowledge and classroom practice to present a variety of strategies to enhance the performance of both boys and girls. While these strategies are grouped together under either reading (Part II) or writing (Part III), based on their primary emphasis, virtually all the activities integrate both and may be applied not only in the context of English language arts but also in other content areas—science, social studies, mathematics, physical education, music and art.

You will note, as you explore *Reading, Writing, and Gender*, that for each activity we describe in detail we have also included variations and extensions. These variations reflect the imagination and intellect of the teachers who took activities from workshops and staff development sessions and made them come alive in their own classrooms. We invite you, too, to revise and refine these activities to meet your own students' needs and inclinations, and to build upon our ideas and suggestions in ways we may not have imagined. So that we may learn from you, we hope you will share your experiences by e-mailing us at ggoldberg@eyeon education.com or broswell@eyeoneducation.com.

We hope this book will not only provide you with some engaging classroom activities but will stimulate your thinking about literacy and gender and enlarge your perspectives toward students' reading, writing, and ways of seeing themselves in the world around them.

# PART ONE

# BOYS AND GIRLS AS READERS AND WRITERS: WHAT WE KNOW

Over the past decade, as we have collaborated on a series of research projects, our goal has always been to use what we have learned about students as readers and writers to improve teaching and learning. During the course of our research, as we immersed ourselves in student responses to both classroom and large-scale assessment activities, over and over again we found our attention veering toward questions about the effects of gender on performance.

Whether we were investigating the significance of students' reading choices or the impact of peer response on students' writing, we would often find ourselves asking each other, "Do you see how the boys keep skipping the first part of this question?" "Why is it that most of the poems seem to be written by girls?" Or, "Have you noticed the way boys write stories with male protagonists, while the girls tend to write stories that feature girls?"

These observations, at first intriguing but tangential to our then ongoing research projects, came to demand investigation in their own right as we found that many questions about students' skills in reading and writing could only be fully understood if gender was taken into consideration. The many questions we had about reading, writing, and gender became even more compelling as we observed a burgeoning popular interest in boys' development (explored in such best sellers as Kindlon and Thompson's *Raising Cain*, 1999, and Pollack's *Real Boys*, 1998), a backlash against efforts toward raising the achievement of girls embodied in such works as Sommers' *The War Against Boys* (2000), and growing public alarm about what has been termed a "new gender gap" in performance. At local, state, and national levels, amassed data demonstrate that boys consistently score significantly lower than girls in measures of reading and writing.

## A NEW GENDER GAP?

The most recent report on reading across grades from the National Assessment of Educational Progress (NAEP), the *1998 Reading Report Card for the Nation and the States*, alerts readers that "as with past assessments, females outperformed males at all three grade levels [4, 8, and 12]." In our home state, Maryland, the long-standing disparity between boys' and girls' performance grew to such proportions that it made headlines in 1999.

A sampling of results from various statewide assessment programs in reading and writing illustrates this disparity:

## Maryland

Data on the Maryland School Performance Assessment Program (MSPAP) are reported in terms of the percentage of students who meet the proficiency level for satisfactory performance on an assessment comprised entirely of constructed response items. The most recent data, presented in the *Maryland School Performance Report* (Maryland State Department of Education, 2000), reveal a consistent difference of at least 10 percent more girls meeting the standard than boys:

|  | *Grade 3* | *Grade 5* | *Grade 8* |
|---|---|---|---|
| **Reading** | M: 34.2, F: 44.4 | M: 38.8, F: 50.5 | M: 19.5, F: 34.4 |
| **Writing** | M: 44.2, F: 55.2 | M: 35.9, F: 48.0 | M: 42.5, F: 61.6 |

## Washington

Data on the Washington Assessment of Student Learning (WASL) are reported in terms of the percentage of students who meet the state's academic standards in core content subjects (OSPI, 2000). In addition to selected response items, the WASL includes brief constructed responses and essays. The most recent data (1999-2000 school year) reveal differences from around 6 percent to over 20 percent between the percentage of girls and boys meeting the standards for reading and writing:

|  | *Grade 4* | *Grade 7* |
|---|---|---|
| **Reading** | M: 63.3, F: 69.5 | M: 38.3, F: 45.8 |
| **Writing** | M: 31.8, F: 48.0 | M: 32.5, F: 54.1 |

## Vermont

Data are reported in terms of the percentage of students meeting or exceeding a satisfactory standard on an assessment comprised of both constructed and selected response for reading and constructed response for writing. Students are assessed at grades 4 and 8, with scores reported for reading analysis/interpretation and basic understanding, and writing conventions and effectiveness. The most recent data (Vermont Department of Education, 2000) reveal differences from 5 percent to as high as 20 percent between the percentage of girls and boys meeting the standard:

|  | *Grade 4* | *Grade 8* |
|---|---|---|
| **Reading: Analysis/Interpretation** | M: 60, F: 69 | M: 21, F: 37 |
| **Reading: Basic Understanding** | M: 80, F: 85 | M: 49, F: 66 |

| Writing: Conventions | M: 40, F: 58 | M: 46, F: 65 |
| Writing: Effectiveness | M: 50, F: 68 | M: 47, F: 69 |

## Kentucky

Data are reported in terms of an average performance index with point values ranging from 0 to 140 assigned to each of eight levels (e.g., novice–nonperformance to distinguished). The most recent data (Kentucky Department of Education, 1999) on reading reveal gender differences of 6 points at the elementary level and 9 points at middle school level.

These data show not only a consistent gap between the performance of boys and girls but also a widening of that gap from grades 3 to 8. Although this gap in reading and writing proficiency in the U.S. has been documented for some time now, the current culture of assessment appears to have ignited wider attention and the demand for instructional intervention. A similar process has been underway for a decade in the United Kingdom, where national test data documenting boys' underachievement in every aspect of the language arts curriculum (Epstein et al., 1998; Ofsted, 1993, 1996) have sparked a considerable body of scholarship concerned with the impact of gender on literacy learning. Thus, what we are witnessing here in the U.S. is not so much a "new gender gap," as it is, for us, a "newly recognized gender gap."

From an instructional rather than an assessment perspective, the issue of boys' lagging achievement is no less obvious, although it is often expressed through anecdote rather than quantifiable data. A quick survey of the past few years' tables of contents or abstracts of journals devoted to reading and writing turns up articles with a clear common denominator. "Literacies and Masculinities in the Life of a Young Working-Class Boy" (Hicks, 2001), "The Silencing of Sammy: One Struggling Reader Learning with His Peers" (Matthews & Kesner, 2000), "Why Does Joshua 'Hate' School…?" (McMillon & Edwards, 2000), and "What Johnny Likes To Read Is Hard to Find in School" (Worthy, Moorman, & Turner, 1999) each associate problematic performance in literary-based activities with boys. Follow this survey by flipping through the pages of almost any recent book on reading. If you keep track of the names of students who are introduced in case studies or close-ups, you are likely to discover that far more of them are boys than girls—so much so that the term "reluctant reader" has almost become a code word for "boy."

As we have engaged classroom teachers and instructional leaders in conversation about gender and performance, many of them have responded by expressing recognition of this phenomenon; they often remark that the data substantiate a felt sense—one they had not articulated before—that girls are leaders in literacy activities. Even as these educators acknowledge the pervasiveness of differences between the performance of boys and girls in English language arts, they share our frustration with long-standing explanations for these differences. All agree it is time to get past theories and "truisms" such as:

♦ girls develop faster than boys

- boys are more active and "hands-on" so reading and writing—solitary and seat-based activities—don't appeal to them

- boys have shorter attention spans

- girls do better because the majority of teachers are women, and they relate better to girls than to boys

Although each of these perceptions may contain some degree of truth, more to the point is that each is inadequate—failing either to explain gender differences in performance or to point toward practical strategies for addressing those differences and bolstering the performance of all students as readers and writers.

# PROFICIENCY IN
# READING AND WRITING

It is significant that evidence of disparity in performance by gender, and teachers' sensitivity towards that disparity, has been growing in tandem with a mounting consensus that reading is best understood as a process of constructing meaning by interacting with text in a variety of ways, along with the general acceptance of a process-oriented approach to the teaching of writing. Only within the context of contemporary understandings of what it means to be a proficient reader and writer can we make sense of differences in how boys and girls interpret and compose texts.

What does it mean to be a proficient reader? In the primary grades, we seek for our students to understand and "unlock" the sound-symbol system, to be able to decode, and to demonstrate basic comprehension of the texts they read. By grade 3, however, expectations widen to include the ability to construct, extend, and examine meaning, and to do so when reading a variety of texts for a variety of purposes. Increasingly, we challenge students not only to read the lines, but also to read between and beyond the lines. They must be able to demonstrate a global understanding by forming an initial, overall impression of the text, develop interpretations, and connect ideas within and across texts and also between text and personal ideas and prior knowledge (Langer, 1989, 1990; National Assessment Governing Board, 1992). Proficient reading also entails the ability to adopt a critical stance—to step back to analyze rhetorical choices and examine how meaning is made. Perhaps most important, as students learn not only to read but to talk (and write) about text, they must develop the ability to leave "footprints in the snow"—evidence that they've entered into and drawn ideas, information, and impressions from the particular text they've read.

Current thinking about reading also acknowledges that readers interact with texts in different ways depending on their purpose for reading. They may read for aesthetic reasons—sometimes described as "reading for literary experience"—and concern themselves not only with ideas, but also with images and feelings. Literary genres such as stories, novels, poems, plays, fables and fairytales lend themselves to reading for this purpose.

Alternatively, readers may interact with texts to acquire information and a greater understanding of a topic or issue. Louise Rosenblatt (1978), whose work has powerfully shaped contemporary approaches to reading, chose the term "efferent," from the Latin word meaning "to carry away," to describe this purpose for reading. Inside and outside of classrooms, when we read nonfiction books, essays, newspaper and magazine articles, web sites, or encyclopedia entries, we are reading to be informed.

In many instructional and assessment contexts, a further distinction is made between reading information for the purpose of expanding knowledge and understanding, and reading information that is more immediately necessary to determine how to do or make something—sometimes called "reading to perform a task" or "functional reading." When readers interact with text for this purpose, they typically want to understand a process and be able to place that understanding in the context of what they know and can do or wish to do. Directions, manuals, activity books, recipes, science investigations, as well as functional documents like schedules and forms are typically read to perform a task.

What does it mean to be a proficient writer? Although writing demands a complex network of skills, proficiency in writing is usually assumed to include both facility in a range of processes—planning, drafting, revising and editing—and an ability to create texts that are characterized by purposeful development to extend and expand ideas, information, and images; a clear and deliberate organizational plan; attention to audience and to a rhetorical situation; and deliberate choices of language to support the meaning to be conveyed. Central to each of these is the ability to anticipate a reader's beliefs, needs and questions, and to make choices (both on a global scale in terms of organization, and on a micro level in terms of wording) that will contribute to the effectiveness of the text for a presumed reader.

An understanding of what it means to be a proficient writer also requires consideration of purpose. The decisions that writers make about shaping and presenting a topic, their determination of a suitable form, and the means they choose to demonstrate attention to a specific audience, all derive from the purpose they have for creating text. Although student writers can create hybrid forms, and the following distinctions are far from absolute, writers generally write for one of several purposes:

- To express personal ideas, by recounting, reflecting upon, or describing a personal or imaginary experience or perspective based on real or imagined occurrences or observations.

- To inform, and explain or describe something by developing ideas with information drawn from prior knowledge or experience (their own or others').

- To persuade, by identifying and defining a problem or issue and developing a position based on personal and/or factual evidence.

# ASSESSING PROFICIENCY IN READING AND WRITING

For the past decade or so, these frameworks for reading and writing have shaped not only classroom instruction but literacy assessment as well. Following the lead of NAEP, a number of state and local reading assessments are grounded in a definition of reading that goes beyond decoding and basic comprehension to evaluate students' ability to construct, extend, and examine meaning, when reading a variety of texts for a variety of purposes. Students demonstrate their proficiency as readers by responding to constructed response activities (e.g., writing, drawing, diagraming, and completing graphic organizers) either exclusively or in combination with selected response items (e.g., multiple-choice, matching). They may be asked to do such things as summarize a story, identify a problem in a story and a character's response to that problem, interpret the message of a text, or assess the appeal of a story for a given audience. As writers, they are expected to be able to produce a variety of text forms for a variety of purposes—informative, expressive, and persuasive.

# FROM ASSESSMENT TO INQUIRY

The Maryland School Performance Assessment Program (MSPAP), the particular assessment that provided the source material for our research on gender and performance, was designed according to this construct for reading and writing. During testing of students' knowledge and skills in core content areas as well as reading and writing, students at grades 3, 5, and 8 read informational selections and sets of directions as well as literary selections and wrote for all three purposes. The extended writing task was structured to mirror typical classroom practices and, over a two-day period, included opportunities for students to prewrite, draft, confer with a peer, and revise their texts.

For our study, we collected over 100 randomly selected answer booklets at each grade level and systematically analyzed responses to a variety of literacy activities from this statewide assessment, examining how boys and girls:

- ◆ make choices about topic and genre when reading and writing

- ◆ identify or establish points of view

- ◆ perceive, represent, and position characters

- ◆ identify and address conflict and emotion

- ◆ represent and respond to authority and context

- ◆ create and respond to gender stereotypes

We focused on students' responses to one of several stories and a set of poems they were given the option of reading, and on the extended piece of writing each composed on a topic, and in a form, of their own choice. In addition, we examined responses to science, mathematics, and social studies activities that required substantial reading or writing and required that students analyze a text or situation, synthesize data to make a recommendation, or assess the best choice of action among several options.

The central question of our study was, "Do boys and girls respond differently to literacy activities in the context of a large-scale assessment? If so, what are the characteristics and implications of these differences?" Aware that researchers can sometimes simply "find what they're looking for" (Crawford, 1995), our examination of students' responses was gender-blind—that is, we read each set of responses without knowing the respondent's gender. Almost immediately, however, we found ourselves "guessing gender" based on certain patterns of topic and language choices, and we decided to record our predictions. Remarkably, when our examination was complete and we then consulted the student data files for gender identification for the more than 200 students whose responses we had examined at grades 3 and 5, both of us had identified each student's gender correctly 100 percent of the time. The fact that children's gender was "written all over the paper" (through such features as topic and language choices) highlighted for us what our own detailed analyses and the research of others were to confirm—that when reading or writing a text, children are also simultaneously "doing gender."

Frankly, this came as no surprise. As early as kindergarten, when children are first learning to read and write, their stories reflect their exploration of gender roles and appropriation of stereotypes. Vivian Paley, in her book, *Boys & Girls: Superheroes in the Doll Corner*, notes that kindergartners "think they have invented the differences between boys and girls and, as with any new invention, must prove that it works" (1984, ix). Similarly, the students whose work we analyzed did not check their gender outside the schoolhouse door. Even as they were explicitly focusing on recounting a story or crafting a poem, they were also announcing and exploring in subtle—and often not so subtle—ways their sense of themselves as either boys or girls in our culture. In other words, as Davies (1993) has so cogently elaborated, when reading and writing, children are operating out of gender identities, and they are also using the occasion of reading or writing to construct and negotiate those identities in some way.

As we were discovering differences in the responses of boys and girls as readers and writers, we repeatedly asked ourselves, "Which, if any, of these differences might account, at least in part, for the disparity in performance? Which, if any, invite us to rethink language arts instruction and to devise strategies to address the sometimes distinct patterns and preferences of boys and girls?" Throughout the process, we reflected on ways that our findings coincided with, extended, or challenged existing literature on reading, writing and gender. Our research yielded consistent evidence of the manifold differences in the ways boys and girls were interpreting questions, responding to texts, and constructing positions for themselves in the world. What follow are some of the most profound and powerful of our findings.

## You Are What You Read/You Read What You Are

The opportunity we had to explore reading, writing, and gender was shaped from the outset by the fact that our samples were drawn from an assessment in which students were permitted to choose what they wished to read and write about. The reading options were each introduced through a very brief synopsis accompanied by a vignette illustration. One of the most immediate ways we saw children "doing gender" was in the choices they made about which selections to read.

Identifying the main character as a girl was often the "kiss of death" when it came to boys' decisions about which selection to read. For example, when a story about a girl's fears about her first day of school was offered as one of three choices, 52 percent of the girls, but only 16 percent of the boys, chose that option. Across grades, whereas many more boys than girls chose stories that explicitly identified a boy or man as the main character, girls were twice more likely than boys to "cross over" gender lines, a pattern also noted by Barrs and Pidgeon (1998) and Millard (1997). Even when story synopses were "gender neutral," evidence from the illustrations that the selection might be "for and about girls" seemed to cause boys to reject those choices. The one notable exception was that one story accompanied by a picture of an African-American girl was disproportionately chosen by African-American males, suggesting, powerfully, that for many students "race trumps gender."

Significantly, while the whole concept of reading "choice" in the assessment was intended to address, among other things, the different tastes of boys and girls as readers, the more fundamental limitation of choice to literary texts may itself be ignoring one of the most pervasive and well-documented differences in boys' and girls' reading behavior. A number of researchers (Barrs & Pidgeon, 1994, 1998; Millard, 1997; Worthy, Moorman, & Turner, 1999), have recognized that girls differ from boys both in their choices of what to read and in their orientation toward those choices. Girls are much more likely to read for pleasure and to choose literary selections. Boys, in contrast, are more likely to read for utilitarian purposes, and to choose informational texts that enable them to extend their knowledge. Our examination of student responses supported Brownstein's observation (1982) that girls, "live longer in the narratives they read"; in fact, we found that even when reading brief informative and functional pieces in the context of content area activities, girls generally entered more fully into the hypothetical worlds presented in texts and were more likely to use their own ideas, observations, and experiences to construct meaning.

## What You See Is What You Get

As we explored children's responses to reading activities, we repeatedly discovered across grade levels that boys were more likely than girls to focus on the literal elements of action and plot, the more material problems in the stories they had read, and the observable consequences of decisions, whereas girls were more likely to go beyond surface details to comment on the relational and emotional implications of these problems or decisions. These patterns parallel the ones recognized by Bowman in her examination of entries in reading response journals (1992). For example, when asked to identify the problem in a story with an environmental message, the boys tended to say, "The woods were filled with garbage," while the girls said, "The boy had to decide whether to clean up the woods or go hiking with his friends." While boys "read the lines," girls much more often read between and beyond the lines, often identifying the moral or lesson in a story, even when not explicitly cued to do so. In contrast, even when responding to a "moral-based" text like a fable, boys were more likely to adopt an efferent stance and to comment on the informational elements of that text.

Not surprisingly, the stories that many boys crafted were similarly "streamlined," and read as list-like and undeveloped sequences of events. We came to call these texts "then, then, then" stories. When boys' storylines were not simply linear, they seemed to jump from situation to situation with little motivation, logic, or transition—rather like scaling levels in a video game. Each new "level" brought a new set of challenges, bigger, "badder" weapons and more energetic responses, uncomplicated by what came before or might conceivably follow.

Even when engaged in activities in the content areas (science, mathematics, social studies) that were scenario-based (a characteristic of most performance assessments), boys repeatedly manifested this same orientation towards the literal and material, and girls repeatedly showed an orientation towards the underlying significance and relational implications. So, for example, when asked how they might make someone new to their community feel welcome, boys suggested, "Buy pizza," whereas girls offered to introduce the newcomer to friends or show that person around. Similarly, confirming the different orientations to moral reasoning explored by Carol Gilligan (1982), when presented with scenarios in which someone has broken a rule or a promise, boys were more likely to recommend action (often a punishment) whereas girls were more likely to propose communication to remedy the situation.

## Just Say "No"

While boys and girls often said they valued the same qualities in the stories they read—suspense, excitement, and surprise—across grade levels, boys were much more likely than girls to be critical of the texts they read and to note features they disliked, rather than liked. When asked whether they would recommend a particular selection to their peers, boys were far more likely to say "No." Again, a pattern that stood out dramatically in responses to reading was echoed in a number of content area activities: boys were more likely than girls to adopt an oppositional stance and to argue that something was unfair, badly designed, or unworthy of consideration. This stance had an analogue in writing—expressed through an ironic voice and a style or tone that teachers often named "an attitude" and found off-putting. Boys' penchant for adopting a resistant stance has also been recognized by Thomas Newkirk (2000), who explains that boys may perceive sincerity and confession of personal response as attitudes that are feminine, acquiescent, and even threatening. This finding, like a number of others from our study, demands that we, as educators, confront the ways that our expectations and values—and their embodiment in the curriculum—may be gendered and may work against individual students (Hynes, 2000; Millard, 1997).

## The Case of the Disappearing Audience

Not only in activities that were explicitly designed to assess skill in reading and writing, but also in science, mathematics, and social students activities, students were often expected to examine issues and make decisions based on utility or impact. For example, they had to:

♦ determine who might use particular data and how they might do so

♦ consider the impact on others (an individual, small group, or community at large) of a particular event

♦ describe the ways in which an exchange of ideas helped to confirm or change their interpretations of findings

♦ identify alternative perspectives and "put themselves in another person's shoes"

♦ make a recommendation based on someone else's needs

In each instance, students had to consider an "other"—the person or persons who might be involved as collaborators or consumers, actors or audience. Across content areas, the responses constructed by boys revealed a tendency to ignore or underplay the needs and perspectives of others. So, for example, they would analyze data but fail to explain how that data could be applied by others; report on an event but not reflect on its meaning or implications in people's lives; give greater—or even exclusive weight—to their own findings rather than placing them in a wider context. Regardless of grade level, boys often removed themselves from relationships that were implied or even explicit in the activities to which they responded. For example, when called upon to persuade neighbors and community members to continue their patronage of a business or service they were offering, girls emphasized issues of trust and the connection between customers and the service provider, whereas boys were more likely to craft a generic advertisement that focused only on the service and its provider.

## Where's Grandma?

Although it has long been recognized that boys craft stories that focus almost exclusively on male characters, one of our most dramatic findings was boys' tendency to write girls and women out of the stories they read and retold. Even when narratives turned on the actions of female characters, as boys retold those stories they tended to erase female characters and either ignore their actions or attribute them to males, a tendency also manifest in adult literature (Atwood, 1978). For example, when retelling a story in which a young boy witnessed a crime and reported this to his grandmother, who then called the police, a considerable number of boys recounted either that "the boy called the police," or simply that "the police arrived," ignoring or overriding the agency of the grandmother in this story. This pattern is significant and troubling on a number of accounts. In typical reading assessments, in which students must summarize a selection, the omission of critical characters or events contributes to lower scores. Seen apart from assessment contexts and consequences, this behavior suggests that boys are less attentive to multiple points of view in the texts they read—and those they produce as writers. Further, this behavior is indicative of a general and sometimes sexist world view that can have negative consequences in the classroom community and beyond.

Eliminating girls and women from the stories they read can be understood as part of a larger pattern of boys' responses to text. Across all selections and activities, and across all grade levels we examined, girls were more likely than boys to focus on the traits of, and choices made by, more peripheral or "supporting" characters, whereas boys were more likely to concentrate their attention on the actions of a single, usually male, protagonist. In their global and interpretive responses to texts, many boys began nearly every sentence with the protagonist's name or portrayed the protagonist as central—even when describing the actions of others (e.g., "The boy saw two men approaching," vs. "Two men approached"). In contrast, girls' retellings were more multivocal, presenting the perspectives of multiple characters and attributing agency to actors other than the protagonist.

These different orientations may be explained, in part, by recalling that all of us, as readers, bring with us the echoes of other texts we have read each time we enter a new text. For boys, the familiarity with the genre of heroic action tales seems to limit, rather than enhance, their readings by orienting them to a single, linear storyline. For girls, familiarity with romance and stories that end "happily ever after" may lead them to retell the story they wish were told rather than, strictly speaking, the one they actually read (see also Gilbert, 1994).

## You Are What You Write/You Write What You Are

Although many writing assessments require students to respond to a particular prompt, our data on expressive writing was drawn from an assessment that permitted students to write either a story, poem, or play about any topic they wished. We discovered that just as gender was central to students' choices as readers, so it was for them as writers. In a classroom setting, children's topic and genre choices are usually negotiated with teachers (particularly those of boys, who more often pick "messy" topics, as described in Schneider's "No Blood, Guns, or Gays Allowed!: The Silencing of the Elementary Writer," 2001) or determined in response to the social expectations of a peer group (see "Gender Identities and Self-Expression in Classroom Narrative Writing," Peterson, 2001). The assessment gave us a more direct view of students' topic and genre choices, because texts passed directly from individual children's pens (with or without limited feedback from a peer) to unfamiliar, adult readers.

We discovered that even before we had the opportunity to read the expressive texts, themselves, the stories, poems, and plays we read announced the authors' gender through title and topic. At grade 3, while there was considerable overlap in topics chosen by boys and girls, significant differences were already apparent. For example, although both boys and girls enjoyed writing about animals, everyday events and personal interests, more than 10 percent of the girls—but no boys—chose to write about friendship, and almost 20 percent of the boys—but no girls—chose to write about sports. The most popular choice for boys, but rare for girls, was to write a horror or adventure story. In grades 5 and 8, as in grade 3, there was considerable overlap of topic, but again, boys were far more likely to write about sports, adventure, and horrific events, while girls were more likely to write about friendship, romance, or the complexity of family relationships. Notable at grade 8 was the emergence of a new genre and set of topics in which both boys and girls would explore such abstract ideas as peace or the importance of dreams. However, girls were more likely to write in this genre (which accounted for nearly 25 percent of the writing by eighth grade girls), and were more likely to use expressive writing as an occasion to explore issues. Unlike younger writers who sometimes seemed trapped by generic conventions, the eighth grade writers—both girls and boys—seemed more "in charge" of their writing.

Echoing patterns found by Millard (1997) and others, across grades and without exception, boys wrote stories whose primary character or characters were male whereas girls were more likely to "cross over" and to create stories that featured male as well as female characters. In the writing of both boys and girls at grade 8, we noted the emergence of a more three-dimensional world inhabited by characters who sometimes challenged stereotypes (e.g., a short boy who wants to play basketball). Girls, however, were more likely to create characters who were multifaceted and psychologically complex, and to contextualize their stories with references to characters' economic situation and to the presence of divorce, drugs, or mental illness in the landscape of their writing.

Although most of our findings about topics and characters were not unexpected, we did not anticipate the attraction to boys of retelling familiar stories or reworking material from popular culture (episodes of "the Simpsons" or "Family of Five," and modern or fractured fairytales, for example). While some of these retellings lacked much sense of the writer's voice, others took the form of effective parodies or sequels. Despite some teachers' dismissal of the value of such work, our findings were very much in concert with those of a number of literacy researchers—most notably Anne Haas Dyson (1997), Mary Hilton (1996), and Tom Newkirk (2000)—who have identified and celebrated the ways that children adapt, resist, and stretch available words and images, exploiting familiar story lines for their own purposes. Dyson, for example, argues that superheroes are central to many children's social and imaginative lives and that familiarity with narrative structure in film, comics, television, and even video games are rich resources for literacy events.

## Contest Without Context

While demonstrating familiarity with traditional story format (complication/solution, beginning, middle, end), the boys' stories we read were marked by a combination of intensity of action and absence of emotion. Despite their recounting of torture, murder, and encounters with supernatural evil, boys rarely named emotions—in only one quarter of the stories did boys make explicit that a character was scared, relieved, happy, or saddened. Boys generally concentrated on "what happened" in terms of plot or action. They used narrative to explore a protagonist's (and perhaps their own) mastery over the material world and over—and in opposition to—external powerful forces. In their stories, conflict was addressed either with violence or through the power of some outside agency.

Across the Atlantic, Peter Thomas has observed many of the same elements in boys' writing, characterizing their story-writing as "contest without context" (1997, p. 26). Thomas offers the useful metaphor of narrative as vehicle, with the reader as passenger. Boys' stories, he suggests, offer a bumpy ride—all maximum revs, gear shifts, hairpin turns and acceleration, with little attention to why they're taking the trip and who is along with them for the ride. Motivation and feeling seem to be regarded by boys as extraneous or intrusive, and in boys' fiction, "action is virtue; reflection, weakness."

# The Girls Who Never Screamed Again

We discovered that girls' writing, in contrast to boys', was most often characterized by a focus on female protagonists embedded in a web of relationships, and often included elaborate articulation of context. The stories by girls, which often stayed "closer to home" and recounted everyday events rather than great adventures (Adler, 1994), followed more individual plots, described more realistic and less stereotypical characters, and were more likely to incorporate dialogue. Their stories, poems, and plays gave less attention to plot (what is happening) and more attention to what Deborah Tannen (1991) has called the "metamessage," exploring the emotions and relationships attendant to what is happening.

By fifth grade, almost ten percent of the girls in our sample told stories that enacted a process of silencing. These stories took several forms: a girl who vows never again to go down to the basement alone, a girl who promises her family never again to go into the woods, a bunny who no longer wants to romp and stray, and perhaps most overtly—and poignantly—several girls who promise not so sing so loud in the future, in a story titled "The Girls That Never Screamed Again" (see Figure 1 on page 14). In each of these stories, one or more characters learn to reign in excess, domesticate their feelings and desires, police their behavior and limit their actions. These stories confirm that girls' narratives are often concerned less with mastering external forces (the concern of the boys' stories) and more concerned with mastering relationships, the self, and the body.

Stories such as these provide confirmation of the particular risks adolescent girls face, highlighted in Pipher's *Reviving Ophelia* (1994), Orenstein's *School Girls* (1994), The AAUW report *How Schools Shortchange Girls* (1992), and Myra and David Sadker's *Failing at Fairness* (1994). This literature calls attention to the limited and limiting images of girls and women in literature and popular culture, and to classroom practices that may favor boys, making readers aware of the "micro-inequities" that can accumulate to create a crisis of confidence among adolescent girls and to disadvantage female students. Marilyn Frye (1983), for example, explains this notion of "micro-inequities" by way of an image of a birdcage. Although any single piece of wire seems harmless enough and easily avoided, the wires of the birdcage combine to confine the bird and curtail its freedom.

## Add a Princess and Stir

Not surprisingly, just as boys tend to focus upon a single male protagonist in the stories they read, they also craft stories from the perspective of a single male protagonist. While some girls wrote stories with a male protagonist, no boys wrote stories with a female protagonist. Often, in boys' stories, the protagonist is the only named character. Even when their stories involved several characters, they were usually all male and their relationships were rarely named. Girls were more likely to include in their stories multiple points of view, to name ancillary as well as central characters, and to explicitly name relationships.

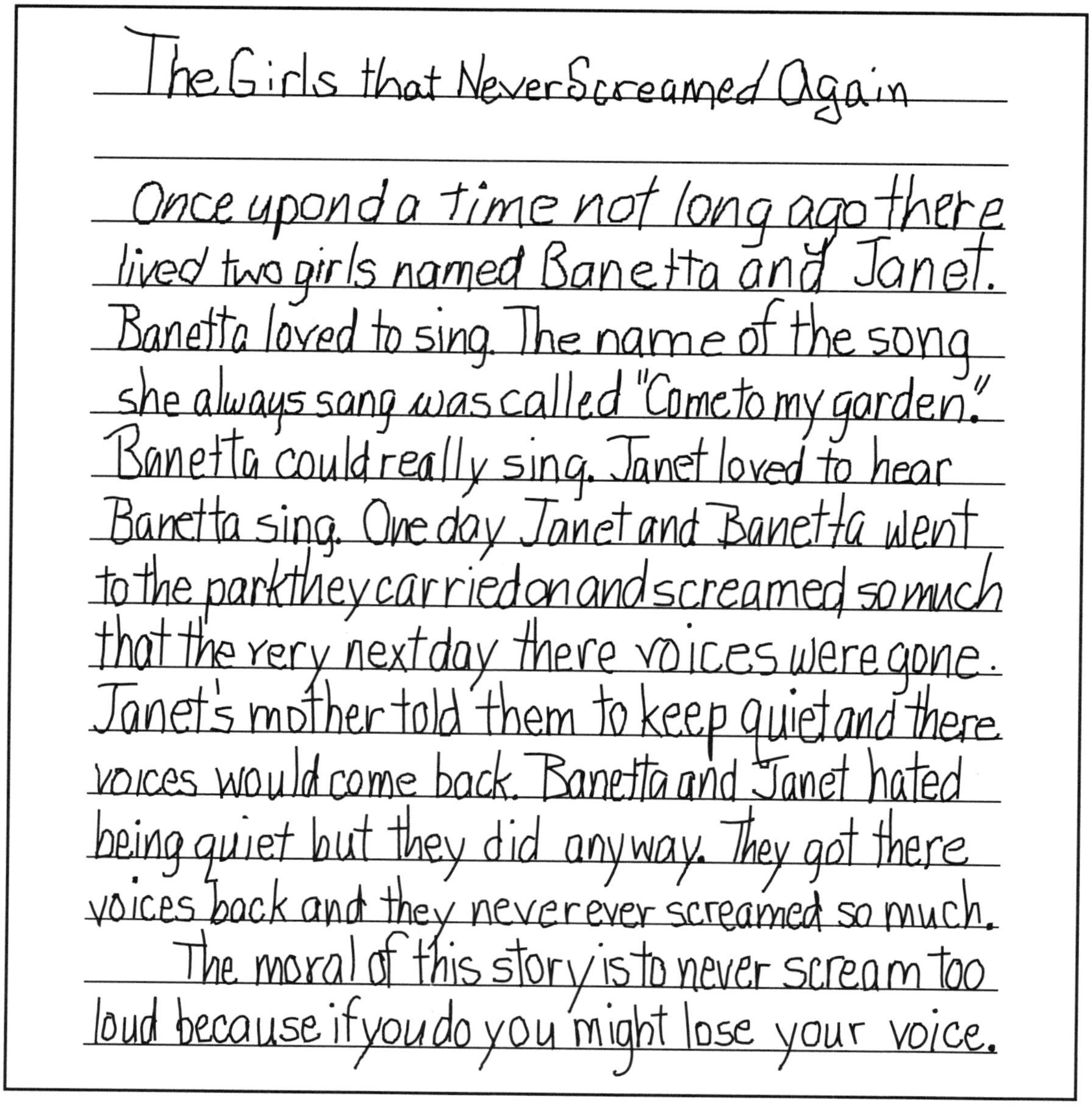

> ## The Girls that Never Screamed Again
>
> Once upon a time not long ago there lived two girls named Banetta and Janet. Banetta loved to sing. The name of the song she always sang was called "Come to my garden." Banetta could really sing. Janet loved to hear Banetta sing. One day Janet and Banetta went to the park they carried on and screamed so much that the very next day there voices were gone. Janet's mother told them to keep quiet and there voices would come back. Banetta and Janet hated being quiet but they did anyway. They got there voices back and they never ever screamed so much. The moral of this story is to never scream too loud because if you do you might lose your voice.

*Figure 1. The process of silencing in a girl's story.*

One extreme and memorable version of this tendency by boys to create worlds inhabited only by men is a story we discovered by a third grader titled "The Dragon and the Man" (see Figure 2 on page 15). The rough draft of the story focused solely on the protagonist's slaying of the dragon. Thanks to the advice the writer received during peer response to "add a princess," however, the final version included a princess victim whose presence served to illustrate the power of the dragon and the bravery of the man. This pattern of including female characters as afterthoughts or accessories (which we came to call "add a princess and stir") was also demonstrated in a fifth grade boy's horror story in which a monster murders a girl, and then the male protagonist successfully kills the monster. The last line of the story reads, *"Everyone lived happily ever after. Except for the girl."*

**Planning**

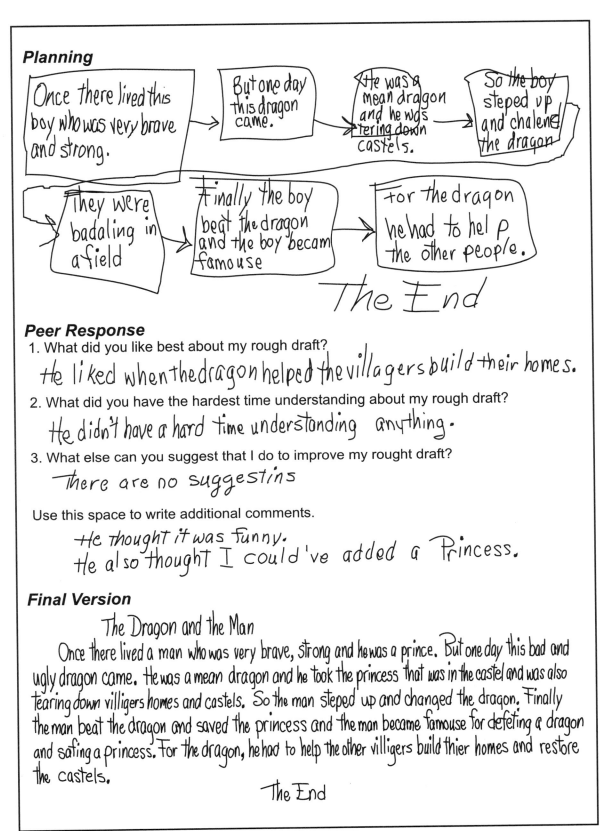

Once there lived this boy who was very brave and strong.

But one day this dragon came.

He was a mean dragon and he was tering down castels.

So the boy steped up and chalenel the dragon

They were badaling in a field

Finally the boy beat the dragon and the boy becam famouse

For the dragon he had to help the other people.

The End

**Peer Response**

1. What did you like best about my rough draft?

He liked when the dragon helped the villagers build their homes.

2. What did you have the hardest time understanding about my rough draft?

He didn't have a hard time understanding anything.

3. What else can you suggest that I do to improve my rought draft?

There are no suggestins

Use this space to write additional comments.

He thought it was funny.
He also thought I could've added a Princess.

**Final Version**

The Dragon and the Man

Once there lived a man who was very brave, strong and he was a prince. But one day this bad and ugly dragon came. He was a mean dragon and he took the princess that was in the castel and was also tearing down villigers homes and castels. So the man steped up and changed the dragon. Finally the man beat the dragon and saved the princess and the man became famouse for defeting a dragon and safing a princess. For the dragon, he had to help the other villigers build thier homes and restore the castels.

The End

*Figure 2. A female character is added as an accessory during the writing process.*

Ironically, these stories share many characteristics with many classics of our culture—stories of the hero and his quest. It is the story of Odysseus, Beowulf, and the Hobbit, of King Arthur and Robinson Crusoe, of Luke Skywalker, Batman, and Indiana Jones, and even of Jack and the Beanstalk, Peter Rabbit, and Max in *Where the Wild Things Are*. It is the ubiquitous story of how a hero (male, sometimes accompanied by male companions) leaves home, ventures into a dangerous wilderness, encounters obstacles and opponents, overcomes these opponents through bravery, resourcefulness, intelligence and determination (often through exercise of justifiable violence, and sometimes with the assistance of wise and benevolent beings who recognize his heroism), achieves his goal, returns home, and is welcomed and rewarded, often with a beautiful woman. Built into the story are a system of binary oppositions (male/female, good/evil, light/dark, reason/emotion, human/nature) that are mutually reinforcing. These stories are told from the hero's point of view, and women in these stories appear only in relation to the hero—as dangerous opponents (witches), as devoted assistants, as victims to be rescued (plot devices), or as prize brides and trophies. When our writer was counseled to "add a princess," his peer was demonstrating his knowledge of the genre and his accurate assessment that including the princess would add to the protagonist's heroism.

Such stories pose particular challenges for girls as both writers and readers. As writers, they can either "write *themselves*," and risk losing half their potential readers, or choose among such alternatives as self-parody, androgyny, or a neutral (almost neutered) public persona. As readers, girls must choose to identify either with the male hero or with the weak or wicked female characters (Fetterley, 1978; Hourihan, 1997). Girls face this quandary even when reading books like the phenomenally popular *Harry Potter* series. J. K. Rowling recently confessed to *Time for Kids* (2000) that her own seven-year old daughter had dressed up like Harry for Halloween. Rowling explained, "I asked her if she didn't want to be Hermione, but she said, 'Harry's cooler.'"

## FROM INQUIRY TO INTERVENTION

Even as these findings were emerging, we began sharing them with teachers, content specialists, and instructional leaders. All of these educators repeatedly responded with the comment that they had noticed similar patterns, but that we had given names to what heretofore had been felt but unspoken. The next set of questions were obvious and urgent: What's next? How can we translate this greater awareness into meaningful classroom instruction?

Believing that students' behavior in the literacy classroom is malleable, we have developed an array of instructional strategies and classroom activities that acknowledge and evolve from the characteristic behaviors of boys and girls when reading and writing. The feedback from teachers and students who have participated in these activities has in turn shaped new ideas and extensions. As you implement these strategies and activities, we hope that you will come to recognize that while boys and girls do read and write differently, they are not, fundamentally, differently able. If we recognize the differences they demonstrate when creating andresponding to text, and then teach with those differences in mind, we can enable children to envision and respond to the wider opportunities available to them as readers and writers, and as they imagine themselves as men and women in the world.

# PART TWO

# BOYS AND GIRLS AS READERS: WHAT WE CAN DO

When it comes to reading, classroom teachers often recognize intuitively the same attitudes and behaviors that researchers (for example Barrs & Pidgeon, 1998; McCracken, 1992; Millard, 1997; Worth, Moorman, & Turner, 1999) have repeatedly documented in recent years. Among these persistent findings about children's reading are that:

♦ overall, boys spend less time reading than girls do and may perceive reading itself as a girls' activity

♦ despite a quarter of a century of attempts at redress, a majority of books available to children continue to reinforce gender stereotypes

♦ boys' and girls' preferences for what they read differ, with boys more likely to choose nonfiction or adventure stories, while girls choose fiction that focuses on characters and relationships

♦ boys select books with a male protagonist and generally resist books with a female protagonist; girls more often select books with a female protagonist but also willingly read books that feature a boy as a main character.

Teachers and researchers have put forth many theories to explain the differences they observe between the interests of boys and girls as readers. Some patterns may arise in response to the reading preferences children see modeled in their families, with boys mirroring their fathers' interest in news, sports, and informational texts, and less often observing men absorbed in the sorts of stories and novels most often assigned and valued in schools (Hicks, 2001; Hynes, 2000; Millard, 1997). Psychological and cultural theories highlight the need preadolescent boys feel to assert independence, to signal their masculinity (especially in peer groups), and to identify with heroic protagonists (Hilton, 1997; Hourihan, 1997). Still other researchers call attention to the many forms that literacy takes in today's culture, urging teachers not to narrow their definitions of literacy in ways that ignore children's sophisticated "reading" of popular culture. They see children's interest in, and familiarity with, television, video, comic books, and even computer games as resources that can inform pedagogy and enrich our teaching of traditional reading and writing (Dyson, 1997; Simmons, 1997).

As a teacher, one of the most important investigations you can undertake is to survey the books you make available to students and uncover your students' reading histories and preferences. Such investigation will help you to better understand your students' individual profiles as readers with particular, often gender-related preferences, strengths, and styles. As Worthy et al. (1999) convincingly explain, recognizing and responding to students' interests as readers is a critical first step in engaging them, creating enthusiasm for reading, and harnessing students' skills to enable them to enter into more challenging texts. On the pages that follow, you will find a set of strategies for inventorying texts and text choices. The information these strategies yield can help you to:

- identify patterns in your own reading choices and in those made by and for your students

- address students' misperceptions about themselves as readers and about reading in general

- recognize the many kinds of "reading" in which boys and girls are already engaged and which can be used to support school literacy

- create a classroom library that includes a balance of texts and will enhance boys' and girls' development as readers

- evaluate texts more systematically and enable your students to do so as well

- offer children ways of monitoring and expanding their own choices as readers.

Differences in reading preferences are only part of the story, however. Listen to the conversations of boys and girls even when they are reading the same text, and it may not be clear to you that they've read and constructed meaning from the same selection. Whether reading fiction or nonfiction, boys and girls often orient themselves to what they've read, and construct, extend, and examine meaning using different strategic tools and with different intentions.

What we know about boys' and girls' different approaches to text points to ways that you can guide your students not only to select, but also to think about and respond to texts of various sorts—literary, informative, and functional—in more varied and effective ways. In addition to the activities that address *what* boys and girls read, we also include in Part II an array of activities that focus on *how* boys and girls read. By engaging students in such practices as supporting negative criticism effectively, attending to multiple points of view and peripheral characters, and analyzing how text features and text structure contribute to meaning, these activities attend to the differing strengths of boys and girls as readers, and encourage all students to respond to what they read with greater complexity and completeness, enthusiasm and insight.

# 1

# ON THE SHELF: INVENTORYING BY THE TEACHER

"What do you like to read?" We often ask children this question as we guide them toward individual reading selections. They may answer, "I like books about sports," identifying a topic that interests them. Other children may identify a preferred genre (science fiction, fantasy, adventure, mystery, biography), a series, or an author whose work they particularly like. Some children may gravitate towards a recurrent theme—surviving trauma or forging a friendship. Their choices may instead be determined by the characters they encounter and the opportunity to identify with a particular protagonist or discover someone like themselves. Underlying these considerations are students' central motivations for reading—to gather information, to gain insight needed to make a decision, to do or make something, and, most often, to be transported to another world and the pleasures of the page.

As teachers, we are very likely to be sensitive not only to this array of criteria, but to several others as well. We may consider the vision of the world that a book puts forth, attending to the place of males and females within that vision, and asking how well the book mirrors the diversity of our classrooms and our world. When children choose what to read, they often ask the obvious question, "Who are the main characters and will I like them?" Those of us who are responsible for creating and shaping opportunities for children to make reading choices may also ask, "What is the point of view and whose voice is telling the story or giving the information?" Fundamentally, we look at a book intended for children and ask, "Who gets to 'name the world' in this book and what sort of world is being named?" Precisely because of our power to shape students' reading choices, we ought to be deeply conscious of what's "on the shelf"—what worlds are available to our students as readers.

Whether the goal is to find appropriate books to meet a particular student's interests, to broaden students' repertoires as readers, or to ensure that the selections we make available mirror the diversity of roles and environments our students confront, a good first step is to inventory the reading selections already at hand in school. You may choose to do this alone, or together with a colleague to gain a wider perspective as you interpret findings.

# CLASSROOM LIBRARY: VISION AND VARIETY

You are very likely to have assembled a classroom library—whether on a shelf in your room or set aside in the school library or media center. Begin your inventory by gathering together a sampling of twelve to fifteen books from this larger set of books you've selected as recommended reading for your students. Consider each title you have gathered and, using a matrix, record a tally mark in each category that describes that title (see "Matrix for Categorizing Reading Selections" on page 21 or use a matrix of your own design).

The matrix we offer has evolved from our recognition that the categories used by many teachers, librarians, and media specialists are sometimes too global or vague, unable to account for hybridization (e.g., a historical novel about the formation of the Negro baseball league and the breakdown of the color barrier in sports). In fact, various researchers who have used surveys to determine students' reading preferences have found such instruments to present limitations (and thus undermine their validity) because of the particular categories provided, which may fuse and confuse topic, theme, and genre (Davies & Brember, 1993; Worthy, Moorman, & Turner, 1999). The benefit of our inventory matrix is its multi-dimensionality, permitting teachers and students alike to describe and categorize reading selections more precisely. Nevertheless, you may note that many titles do not fit neatly into any single category and that there is often overlap. In fact, many favorites (the *Harry Potter* books, for example) go beyond the typical formula for a given genre. For the purposes of this activity, either pick the best "fit" or put a tally mark under all categories that apply.

After quickly filling out the chart for books you have selected, you are likely to gain a new perspective towards the books on your shelves by asking such questions as:

- Based on this matrix, what do I notice about the books I make available to children?

- Is there a preponderance of books in some categories, and an absence in others?

- What generalizations can I make about characters in the books I've inventoried—are they more often children or adults? Male or female?

- Which of these patterns or generalizations were a surprise to me and which were predictable?

The least predictable results are likely to be those regarding point of view and voice: In the books you make available, who is doing the talking and are they talking to and about us or with us? Do any of the nonfiction selections give voice to children or novices and make their experiences credible? Are children telling their own stories or are those stories related by more mature or omniscient narrators?

When Ron, a fourth grade teacher in a suburban school, conducted a classroom library inventory, he discovered:

- a concentration of books in a limited number of genres, often fantasy and realistic fiction

# MATRIX FOR CATEGORIZING READING SELECTIONS

| GENRE | TOPIC | MAIN CHARACTER(S) | POINT OF VIEW |
|---|---|---|---|
| nonfiction | sports | a boy | expert |
| | | | |
| autobiography | animals/nature | a girl | participant (m) |
| | | | |
| mystery | family | a man | participant (f) |
| | | | |
| fantasy/science fiction | friends | a woman | outsider/observer (m) |
| | | | |
| humor | school | group of boys/men | outsider/observer (f) |
| | | | |
| historical fiction | other times/places | group of girls/women | multiple perspectives |
| | | | |
| realistic fiction | other cultures | mixed age/gender | narrator (m) |
| | | | |
| fairytale/folktale | adventure | animal/imaginary-male | narrator (f) |
| | | | |
| poetry | doing/making something | animal/imaginary-female | omniscient/unclear |
| | | | |
| other | other | other | other |
| | | | |

From *Reading, Writing, and Gender* by Goldberg and Roswell (© 2002).
Permission to duplicate for classroom use is granted by Eye On Education, Larchmont, NY.

- the absence of at least some genres, and the small number of biographies and non-fiction titles

- within the limited nonfiction selections, a narrow range of topics, e.g., sports and animals

- the clustering of books about a single protagonist, either male or female and often imaginary or nonhuman

- the dominance of first or third person point of view

For Ron, some implications were obvious and involved filling in a few gaps and widening the array of selections available to students. Unlike the small but orderly clusterings on shelves of volumes of poetry and picture books that he used primarily as writing resources, the shelves of books available for independent reading were jumbled and did little to guide students' choices. In his usual practice of conflating some genre and topic descriptors (for example, sports and biography), Ron recognized that he had missed opportunities to widen and deepen readers' perspectives and build upon their passions for certain kinds of books. As a result of the fresh perspective he gained by reflecting on the categories in the matrix—especially point of view—Ron intended to widen the dimensions he considered when recommending reading selections in the future.

The implications you draw from your own inventory may provide similar food for thought and whet your appetite for some other ways to examine what's on your shelves.

**NEXT STEPS:** After conducting the overview inventory, you may wish to repeat the process, now focusing on the books most typically chosen by boys and girls. Select six to eight books that are top choices of boys and another six to eight most often chosen by girls. There may be overlap with the first set of books you inventoried. Using two different colored pens or pencils to differentiate between boys' and girls' choices, repeat the inventory process for these titles.

Take the time to reflect upon what you notice about the similarities and differences between the first and second inventory:

- How does the second chart differ, if at all, from the first one?

- Are any categories of books consistently selected by both boys and girls?

- What do the patterns you note tell you about the children you teach?

- What do they tell about your own preferences and assumptions? Do your selections look much like those of children the same sex as you?

Your preliminary inventorying is likely to bring to the fore some findings that heighten your sensitivity to issues related to gender. The next approach to inventorying therefore focuses more directly on the vision of the world—and specifically the way men and women are portrayed—in the books to which children are exposed.

# MEN AND WOMEN
# IN THE WORLDS WE READ

As parents and teachers, our generation was the first to have available a growing body of children's literature that attempted to go beyond stereotypes and to portray men and women in a variety of contexts and roles. For example, women were no longer portrayed as homebound and vulnerable, and men were portrayed in more nurturing roles. Girls were seen engaged in challenging and risk-taking activities and as effective problem solvers, whereas boys might be seen engaged in expressive and relational activities. Despite these attempts, the majority of works of children's literature continues to present a more traditional and stereotypical vision of the world.

To begin your analysis using this inventory strategy, first reflect back upon selections you have shared with your students. These may be books or stories that you have read aloud, that students have read along with you, or that you have assigned or recommended for partnered or independent reading. List ten to fifteen of these, and then code as "A," "B," or "C," titles that fall into the following categories:

**Category A: Stories that convey traditional ideas about gender roles/identities**

In these stories, the problem solvers are usually boys or men who are active in the world. Women may be absent, portrayed as victims, or confined to limited, often domestic roles. These stories usually end with order restored and people all "in their place." Such stories may be considered to perpetuate gender stereotypes. Traditional fairy tales, folktales and legends epitomize such selections.

**Category B: Stories with an explicit feminist message**

Central to the theme of these stories is the message that girls can be independent and active, often engaging in traditionally "male" enterprises like sports or science. Boys, conversely, may be represented in nurturing roles such as child care and engaged in domestic arts such as cooking or sewing. Such stories may be considered to reverse, or conspicuously play upon, stereotypes. Some familiar examples are *Oliver Button is a Sissy* (De Paola), *Sam Johnson and the Blue Ribbon Quilt* (Ernst) and *The Paper Bag Princess* (Munsch) for young readers and Tamora Pierce's *Alanna* series (*The First Adventure*, *In the Hand of the Goddess*, *The Woman Who Rides Like a Man*, and *Lioness Rampant*) for older readers.

**Category C: Stories without an explicit feminist message but with nonsexist roles/identities**

Without comment or apology, some stories feature both male and female characters engaged in a range of activities and environments including those traditionally assigned to the other gender. They succeed in reducing and challenging stereotypes and offering a nonsexist view of the world without gender being a primary focus. We particularly like *Three Days on a River On a Red Canoe* (Williams), *Miss Rumphius* (Cooney) and the *Cam Jansen* mystery series (Adler) for younger students and *Harriet the Spy* (Fitzhugh) and the books of Karen Cushman (*Catherine, Called Birdy, The Midwife's Apprentice,* and *Matilda Bone*) for older ones.

Once again, ask yourself, "What do I see and what does it mean? Which findings surprise me and which confirmed my expectations?"

If you're looking for more selections with characters who "break the mold," you may wish to consult the May 1999 "Talking About Books" Column in *Language Arts*, titled "Strong Female Characters in Recent Children's Literature." Insistent in their emphasis on literature of quality first, and fresh representations of gender second, the authors Heine and Inskster provide an excellent schema ("Six Characteristics to Consider when Examining Children's Books for Positive Gender Role Models," p. 229) for evaluating selections for the portrayal of worthwhile male and female role models and for thoughtful representations of gender in children's books.

---

# Looking Deeper

As you try to categorize books in terms of their representation of gender, you may find yourself struggling because some stories are too complex to fit neatly into category A, B, or C. For example:

♦ In *Princess Furball* (Huck), the princess rejects the suitor chosen by her father, and she protects herself through disguise and strategy. Nevertheless, the story ends with a very traditional wedding—complete with prince and white gown—that restores the princess to the role of compliant beauty, wife, and mother. (Intermediate)

♦ In *Insects are My Life* (McDonald), we meet Amanda, a budding entomologist. Although we admire her confidence and intelligence, it seems unfair that this brainy bug expert has to be pudgy, brunette, and bespectacled. One stereotype has been overturned, but other, more stubborn ones, are reinforced. (Intermediate)

♦ In the inaugural volume in the *Scrappers* series, *Scrappers #1: Play Ball!* (Hughes), recreation council deadlines and some registration glitches lead Robbie and Trent to recruit two girls in order to form a new baseball team. Through a series of trials, the members learn to cooperate and work as a team, growing in various ways as individuals and becoming more supportive of each other—yet not without characters' frequent descriptions of each other's skills as pretty good "for a girl" or "for a boy," reinforcing certain stereotypes even as the book attempts to challenge them. (Intermediate–Middle School)

♦ In *True Confessions of Charlotte Doyle* (Avi), we follow the protagonist as she faces a number of extraordinary challenges while crossing the Atlantic in 1832 without the protection or supervision of any adults in general, or men in particular. Unlike so many female protagonists in tales of adventure, Charlotte does not compromise her female identify through disguise, although she winds up aspiring to a distinctly male lifestyle—seafaring. (Middle School)

**NEXT STEPS:**

- Check and record the original date of publication of the books you've selected. How have representations of gender roles and contexts changed over time? Did you find, as did some teachers we know, that more recently published books are more likely to reduce and challenge stereotypes in subtle and realistic ways than to simply say "It's our turn now" and combat stereotypes by reversing them?

- Consider which were easier to find—books that portrayed girls in nontraditional roles and activities or books that portrayed boys in a comparable way? There is reason to believe that children's literature still features more female astronauts and explorers than male nurses or kindergarten teachers, and we may be offering more opportunities to girls than boys to overcome limitations and ignore stereotypes.

- Narrow the field to booklists such as the last two decades' Caldecott or Newberry Award winners, or to other published lists of recommended reading selections. Do you see any differences in the patterns that emerge when categorizing these selections? What do these differences suggest to you?

- Consider the ways in which recent children's films and television programs similarly treat gender in complex and often contradictory ways. Disney films like *Beauty and the Beast*, for example, may step beyond the traditional portrayal of a damsel in distress while holding fast to the basic message and story line of a fairy-tale world.

# TEACHERS AS READERS

Think of some of the books you have read over the last year or two and jot down their titles. Return to a matrix for categorizing reading selections and now fill out the matrix based on your own personal reading selections. What do you notice? How congruent are your personal choices with those you offer in your classroom or with those of the individual students you teach?

Write a few paragraphs reflecting on the patterns you notice. Here is what one teacher said when she did this:

> When I think about the books I've read over the last year, I see that I am mostly drawn not only to fiction, but to fiction written by female authors that focuses on family and relationships, usually with female protagonists—"Oprah books." I also see that some of the books that I've enjoyed most are the couple I've read by male authors that maybe take me further out of myself and introduce points of view more different than my own. In addition to books I read for work, I also often seek out advice books—on child rearing, time management, home renovation. I seem to go to books for general advice (maybe to get a sense of control?) when I am confronting a challenge in my personal life.

# REVISITING OLD FRIENDS

Think about a children's/young adult book that was a particular favorite when you were in grades 3–8, or that you particularly love to teach or to recommend to children. What do you notice when you characterize it? One teacher who did this noted:

> Norton Juster's *The Phantom Tollbooth* was a favorite when I was a child, and I have enjoyed sharing it with countless children since. I love the puns, the whimsy, the celebration of the imagination—who can forget the descriptions of being stuck in the Doldrums or of conducting a sunrise symphony of color? But when I looked at the book again today, I noticed some new things about it: all the main characters are male, and the few female characters are either evil or, despite their benign names like "Rhyme" and "Reason," pretty typical damsels in distress. It is really a fairy-tale–quest story, and in the end the hero must use violence to achieve his goal. I remember loving the story, yet never really identifying with Milo, and I think that now I might have a sense of "why."

And another teacher recalled:

> I was just rereading Munch's little picture book *The Paper Bag Princess*. It recounts the tale of a princess who, wearing only a paper bag, outsmarts the dragon who has captured Ronald the Prince and manages to free Ronald. He in turn, ungenerously responds by criticizing the princess's disheveled appearance, and the book closes with her telling Ronald off and joyfully dancing off into the sunset alone. The book is funny and refreshing, and I would continue to offer it to students. But I'm a little disturbed not only by its direct reversal of traditional fairy tales, but also by its either/or logic and its implications that if a woman (a princess!) is too strong and independent, she may have to renounce love and live alone.

As in life, revisiting old friends is not just pleasurable but may bring unexpected insights and a tempering of earlier enthusiasms or anxieties. The experience of revisiting may better prepare us as we enter into new relationships—whether with people or with books.

# 2

# OFF THE SHELF: INVENTORYING BY AND WITH STUDENTS

Just as teachers can learn a great deal by inventorying, students also can be recruited in the effort to learn more about themselves as readers by examining the choices they make. The activities that follow present different ways for students—individually and as a class—to reflect on their interests and habits as readers. The following activity, "Reading Celebrities," honors and makes public children's often hidden or unacknowledged interests and skills as readers. Students participate in an interview with a family member to create a reading autobiography, and then contribute to a live or videotaped presentation on "Reading Celebrities." Inviting students and their families to reflect on all their reading, in school and outside of school, brings the often self-sponsored but "discounted" reading of nonfiction and pop culture sources into the classroom where it can enrich literacy learning.

## READING CELEBRITIES

**HOW TO GET READY:** Prepare and send a letter home to inform parents, guardians, and/or older siblings of the need for every student to have a partner to conduct the celebrity interview. A sample letter might read:

> Popular television and radio programs often include interviews with celebrities—people who are famous because of special things they have done or achieved. Our class is planning to create a program on "Reading Celebrities," to highlight the special interests and experiences that helped make each student a star as a reader. Please have someone in your home take a few minutes to interview _____ _____ about his or her reading. Listen and record the answers to each question.

Include a copy of the interview form with this letter (see pages 28–29).

**SUGGESTED GROUPING:** individual, pairs, and whole group

# Interview With A Reading Celebrity

Celebrity's name_____

Interviewer's name _____

1.  What are some of the first reading experiences you remember?

_____

_____

_____

2.  What kinds of reading in school/for school do you enjoy?

_____

_____

_____

3.  How do you think other people (teachers, classmates, parents, friends) would describe you as a reader?

_____

_____

_____

_____

4.  When you read outside of school, what sorts of things do you read? (e.g., magazines, catalogues, etc.)

_____

_____

_____

5.  Who, if anyone, do you like to talk to about what you have read?

_____

_____

_____

6. Even reading celebrities don't spend all their time reading. When you watch television, what programs do you enjoy?

_____

_____

_____

7. If you play computer games, which ones do you enjoy?

_____

_____

_____

8. How would you say these activities (watching television and playing computer games) are like and/or unlike reading?

_____

_____

_____

*TO THE INTERVIEWER:* What is the most interesting or important thing you found out about your reading celebrity? Please circle that response above.

Any other questions? Record your questions and the responses to them below.

***Thank you for helping by interviewing your reading celebrity!***

**HOW TO INTRODUCE THE ACTIVITY (SAY/DO):** "How many of you have ever seen or heard someone being interviewed? What is an interview?" (Engage in discussion, eliciting the idea that in an interview, someone asks questions of another person to learn more about his or her interests, experiences, and talents).

"When you go home today, please give this letter to an adult in your household. It contains directions for conducting an interview with you. Something that I think is special about you is that you are all reading celebrities—there are special facts about you as a reader that would be interesting to others. Over the coming days, we will share these interviews with each other, and combine the most interesting parts in a [live program, videotape, audiotape] to share [over the public address system, closed-circuit television, on stage] with [other students, family members]."

**HOW TO DO THE ACTIVITY:** When students have brought in their completed Celebrity Interviews, have them first take turns identifying the response that was circled by their interviewers when asked, "What is the most interesting or important thing you found out about your celebrity as a reader?" See if any patterns emerge (both in terms of most frequently circled questions and students' responses to those questions) and suggest that these might become the focus of the class presentation. Then discuss with students other possible ways in which various questions and answers might be grouped to provide a theme or focus to the presentation. For example, the host might read a given question and then solicit responses to that question from three of four students for whom that was the most interesting or important.

Once a plan for the presentation has been agreed upon, assign students to serve as the show hosts or ask for volunteers. Students can take turns passing the microphone so that everyone gets to make a guest appearance as a reading celebrity and has an opportunity to respond to at least one question. Encourage students to ad lib with comments, exclamations, and extensions to ideas, perhaps probing to find out, "What made you say that?" Students may even wish to add as "commercials" during the final presentation brief synopses of some favorite books. After sufficient rehearsal, you'll be ready to roll the audio- or videotape or conduct a live presentation.

Although students will certainly enjoy the production aspects of this activity, its true purpose is to get students thinking about themselves and others as readers, and to make discoveries and connections along the way. Some students who tend to think of themselves as nonreaders may reconsider this notion as they reflect on how much functional reading (manuals, directions, data displays) they actually do. They may discover and consider the implications of continuity or discontinuity between school- and home-based reading activities. Through their reading celebrity interviews, students are likely to discover how very strong their memories of learning to read are, and how deeply tied those memories are likely to be to particular people both in and outside of school.

# CREATING A COMMUNITY OF READERS

Among the most consistent findings from researchers is that successful readers enter more fully into the world of the books they read and talk with other readers about texts. In a sense, both "living in the story" and letting "stories live in you" are ways of connecting textual worlds and social worlds, making more permeable the boundaries between life and text, self and other. Not only do proficient readers "stay longer" in the world of the book by relating to characters, envisioning elements of the story, and connecting the story to their own lives, but proficient readers are also more likely to recommend books to friends and seek recommendations from others, to discuss characters and events in a story with other readers (almost as a form of gossip), and to relate a story to others they have read.

Readers often share what they have read without writing formal reviews. To support the creation of a community of readers in your classroom, divide your class into four groups. Once every two weeks, invite each of the students in one of the groups to present a book talk about a book they have read during the past month. Prepare students by discussing strategies to pique interest without spoiling the suspense or "giving away" the ending. Many students will welcome the opportunity to draw on what they know about movie or television previews to suggest ways to "preview" a book for classmates.

Numerous teachers who have worked successfully with reluctant readers have found that an effective way to generate enthusiasm for reading is to have students use the occasion of the book talk to give "performative readings" of short passages from a book. Students choose a passage that they believe will give others the flavor of the book or will entice others to read the book. Students then "perform" this passage, reading it aloud with expression and attention to the most effective ways (though pacing, volume, pitch, etc.) to represent different character's voices. Many of the critical skills we hope to develop in readers—the ability to identify key passages, to analyze character, and to create an empathetic bond with a person in a world different from one's own—are involved in this "pencil-free" and nonthreatening reenactment of a short scene from a book. You may choose to organize students in pairs, so that students can coach each other as they plan and rehearse.

The basic notion of a book talk or performative reading opens the door to countless variations (see Wilhelm, 1997), many of which can be used not only for students to share independent reading, but also can be incorporated into discussion of a class text. These include writing and performing a missing (but implied) scene from the book, offering a "newscast" of the late-breaking events in the plot, or writing (and then reading aloud) correspondence from a character—perhaps in the form of a letter or an e-mail exchange. In each case, a focus on experimentation, collaboration, and performance, rather than written text as artifact, will enable all students to engage with texts more fully.

# VARIATIONS/EXTENSIONS

## A Reading Celebrity's Autobiography

Instead of focusing on the creation of a "Reading Celebrities" presentation, students may wish to use the information gathered during their interview to compose autobiographies of themselves as readers. These accounts will help both you and your students recognize their unique preferences and abilities. You may learn, for example, that a student who seems unengaged in "school reading" is an avid reader of a specialty magazine (*Sports Illustrated, American Girl, Nintendo Power*) or that a particular student is an expert game player whose understanding of visual cues, stock characters, and plot conventions can be used to develop her or his abilities to analyze and interpret the kinds of written texts usually assigned in school.

## What Did You Read Today?
## (A Day in the Life of a Reading Celebrity)

Ask your students to keep a log of everything they read on a given day: cereal boxes, newspapers, circulars from stores, directions to make or do something, a favorite Web site, a note from a parent or friend—not just books, and not just what they read during school hours. Have students compare these lists in groups or in a whole class discussion. You might ask:

♦ What surprised you about someone else's list?

♦ How is the reading you do at home different from the reading you do in school?

♦ What do you notice about what you can do as a reader that you had not noticed before?

## Reading Detective

This activity is a variant of the one above—in this case, however, instead of keeping a personal record, students are asked to put on a "reading detective's hat" and find people "caught" in the act of reading. What sorts of things do people read? How often are different people "caught?" When is reading a public act, and when is it a private one?

## Magazine Exchange

With the help of your school librarian or media specialist, gather a varied assortment of magazines published for young readers. Some titles that are widely available are *Highlights, Nickelodeon, Time for Kids, Girl's Life, Boy's Life, Ranger Rick, Sports Illustrated for Kids, Cobblestone, Odyssey* and *Calliope*. Give students a chance to look through the collection and then each select and skim through one magazine that appeals to them. Then have students pair up with a classmate of the opposite sex and trade magazines. Give each pair the opportunity to discuss their magazine choices—what did they choose to read, and why? Would they anticipate that someone of the opposite sex would enjoy the same magazine (why or why not)?

What, if anything, about the magazine signaled that it was more of a "boys' magazine" or a "girls' magazine?"

The magazine exchange is even more engaging if your students are able to bring in a magazine or newspaper that is often read either by themselves or by an older friend or family member of the same sex (but no X-rated magazines, though please!). This may be a magazine or newspaper to which someone routinely subscribes or an issue that has been borrowed (from a local library or a friend). Now you're likely to see titles like *Wrestlemania, Young Rider, Dirt Bike, Pokémon, Seventeen, People,* and *Nintendo Power.* Again, have students trade periodicals so that boys and girls get to examine the sorts of reading selections they each favor. As you guide students' discussion of interesting observations, try to get beyond differences in topics (what articles are about) to differences of format and presentation (how information is conveyed). Students may note differences in article length and format, or in the relationships between text and images, copy and advertisements. Again, ask, "What, if anything, signals that this periodical is intended primarily for boys/men or girls/women?" "What might publishers do to change these perceptions and widen their audience?"

If you are able to do both magazine exchanges (school- and home-based resources), you may wish to extend discussion to whether one set of periodicals is more gendered than the other or to other generalizations the students can make about magazines and their intended readers.

# 3

# A MATTER OF CHOICE/ CHOICE MATTERS TO READERS

Because it is essential to students' success as literacy learners that they see themselves as part of a community of readers, the inventorying of reading choices by both teachers and students themselves is critical. It allows teachers and students to identify and honor the full range of students' literacy experience—with academic and popular texts, with reading both in and outside the schoolhouse. At the same time, building on the acknowledgment of each student's individuality as a reader, inventorying may provide the impetus for them to broaden their reading repertoires. One approach to inventorying that is particularly useful in this regard is to chart choices. Although many students keep (or have kept) reading logs, rarely are they asked to go beyond recording and briefly responding to what they read to reflect on the patterns in reading choices the log reveals. By identifying and analyzing patterns in their own reading, students can form some alternate plans and increase the range and variety of choices they make as readers.

## CHARTING READING CHOICES

HOW TO GET READY: Give each student a copy of the "Charting Choices Matrix" on page 36. An alternative is to first brainstorm with your students ways of characterizing reading selections and use student-generated categories (such as topic, genre, theme or "main idea," main character(s), and point of view) to create a matrix unique to your classroom comunity for each student to use.

SUGGESTED GROUPING: individual

HOW TO INTRODUCE THE ACTIVITY (SAY/DO): "Have you ever heard the expression 'creature of habit?' What does that expression mean to you?" (Engage in discussion, leading to the idea that in some ways, people tend to do the same things, the same ways, or make the same choices).

"Over the course of the next few weeks and months, we are going to see if we are 'creatures of habit' when it comes to reading. We'll be charting choices we make as readers, to see if we tend to pick the same genres or types of reading selections, such as mysteries or science fiction, the same topics, such as sports or animals, or pick reading selections that are similar in

# CHARTING CHOICES MATRIX

| GENRE | TOPIC | MAIN CHARACTER(S) | A POINT OF VIEW |
|---|---|---|---|
| non-fiction | sports | a boy | expert |
| biography | animals | a girl | participant (m) |
| mystery | family | a man | participant (f) |
| fantasy/ science fiction | friends | a woman | outsider/ observer (m) |
| humor | school | group of boys/men | outsider/ observer (f) |
| historical fiction | other times/places | group of girls/ women | multiple perspectives |
| realistic fiction | other cultures | mixed age/gender | narrator (m) |
| fairytale/folktale | adventure | animal/ imaginary-male | narrator (f) |
| poetry | doing/ making something | animal/imaginary- female | omniscient/ unidentifiable |
| other | other | other | other |

color key        title of selection                    author                    date completed

❏ _____

❏ _____

❏ _____

❏ _____

❏ _____

❏ _____

From *Reading, Writing, and Gender* by Goldberg and Roswell (© 2002).
Permission to duplicate for classroom use is granted by Eye On Education, Larchmont, NY.

some other way. Once we see if any patterns emerge, our challenge will be to become more adventuresome, and depart sometimes, in some ways, from our usual paths as readers."

**HOW TO DO THE ACTIVITY:** To begin charting, have students color code a recent reading selection. Using a crayon, marker, or colored pencil, have them draw a line connecting the descriptors that characterize that selection according to the headings noted. These lines will most likely look like erratic line graphs as they zigzag across the chart. When more than one entry in a column fits, lines may "branch" and then reconnect (for a sample completed matrix see Figure 3.1 on page 38).

Each time students finish reading a self-selected book or magazine, remind them to chart that choice. After about five or six choices have been charted, suggest that each student share his or her chart with a classmate and discuss any interesting patterns they observe together.

- ♦ Is either of them a "creature of habit" when it comes to choosing what to read?

- ♦ Is there one or more habitual choice? That is, does either reader tend to stick to one or two particular genres? To one or two particular topics? To books and stories with characters who frequently seem to be the same age and/or gender ?

As students talk with their partners, you may wish to circulate to gain a sense of students' choices and perceptions and to stimulate discussion. After students have sufficient opportunity to examine patterns, announce a charting-choice challenge. Based on any patterns students have seen emerge, ask that the next time they choose something to read, they pick a selection that is different from their usual choices in at least one way. Students will probably feel more comfortable making one change at a time (let's say, venturing into a new topic), but some will enjoy the "mega-challenge" of picking a selection that is as different as it can possibly be. Thus, the boy who typically chooses humorous books and magazine articles about people his own age and in similar settings, written from the perspective of a male outsider/observer, may decide to "take the plunge" and pick a work of historical fiction, set in another time and place, involving a complex set of male and female characters of varying ages, told from the perspective of a female narrator. On the other hand, the girl who loves fairy tales and folktales from other cultures, told from the perspective of an omniscient narrator, may take a completely new path by choosing an autobiography of a female sports figure.

The matrix in Figure 3.1, completed by Barbara's sixth grade son, highlights Michael's general enthusiasm for literature and his interest in reading across a number of genres (from autobiography and nonfiction to realistic fiction, historical fiction and fantasy). Nevertheless, a majority of the books he records focus on adventure and survival tales; without exception, the books he has chosen have men and boys as the main characters and are told from the point of view of a man or a boy. Even a reader as ambitious and versatile as Michael can benefit from encouragement to consider other genres, and especially, to seek out some books with female protagonists. Charting his reading choices enabled Michael's teacher to honor his attraction to stories of adventure and survival and also to take advantage of his enthusiasm for the work of Jane Yolen and his interest in the holocaust. Michael's teacher directed him not only to *Maus I and II* (Speigelman's recounting of his father's survival in comic book form),

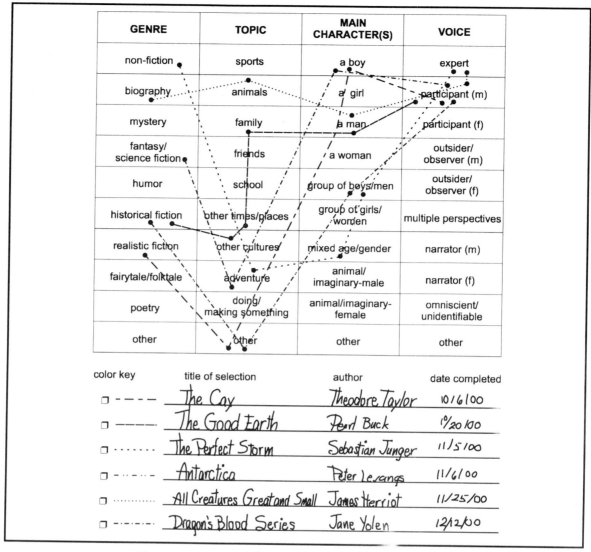

| GENRE | TOPIC | MAIN CHARACTER(S) | VOICE |
|---|---|---|---|
| non-fiction | sports | a boy | expert |
| biography | animals | a girl | participant (m) |
| mystery | family | a man | participant (f) |
| fantasy/ science fiction | friends | a woman | outsider/ observer (m) |
| humor | school | group of boys/men | outsider/ observer (f) |
| historical fiction | other times/places | group of girls/ women | multiple perspectives |
| realistic fiction | other cultures | mixed age/gender | narrator (m) |
| fairytale/folktale | adventure | animal/ imaginary-male | narrator (f) |
| poetry | doing/ making something | animal/imaginary-female | omniscient/ unidentifiable |
| other | other | other | other |

| color key | title of selection | author | date completed |
|---|---|---|---|
| ☐ - - - - | The Cay | Theodore Taylor | 10/6/00 |
| ☐ ——— | The Good Earth | Pearl Buck | 10/20/00 |
| ☐ - - - - - - | The Perfect Storm | Sebastian Junger | 11/5/00 |
| ☐ - - · - · | Antarctica | Peter Lerangs | 11/6/00 |
| ☐ ·········· | All Creatures Great and Small | James Herriot | 11/25/00 |
| ☐ - · - · - | Dragon's Blood Series | Jane Yolen | 12/12/00 |

*Figure 3.1 A completed Charting Choices Matrix.*

but also to Yolen's *The Devil's Arithmetic* (in which a contemporary Jewish girl travels through time and finds herself in a small Jewish village in Nazi-occupied Poland soon destined for Auschwitz) and to Winter's *Katarina* (a story of a Slovakian girl who spends the war disguised, hidden, and in flight).

By providing a concrete record of reading choices, students' charts can become a sort of "road map" to guide their reading, as well as a stimulus to dialogue between teacher and student. Students may wish to stop periodically, to evaluate the matrix itself, and see if there are other headings they wish to add or substitute for the ones on the original form.

Instead of making "Charting Reading Choices" an ongoing activity, you may wish to use it as an opening activity in the fall by asking students to record books they recall reading over the summer and the previous year. In addition to prompting students to reflect on their recent reading histories, the charts will help you get to know your students' interests quickly and enable you to better guide their reading choices. Another alternative is to ask your students to "chart choices" midyear, in order to establish some goals and determine a reading plan for the upcoming months.

# VARIATIONS/EXTENSIONS

## Reading Choices Bingo

You may wish to encourage students to depart from their usual choices by structuring the reading challenge as "Reading Choices Bingo," using some of the choice categories and options to create a bingo board (see page 40 for sample). Students' self-selected reading choices may then be guided, though not overly constrained, by these options. An appropriate prize such as a book or magazine may be awarded to the first student in a given time span (e.g., within the month) whose reading choices create a horizontal, vertical, or diagonal line in the reading-bingo board. When charting choices, through this or another means, the reading-writing connection is a natural one (see Chapter 15, "A Matter of Choice/Choice Matters to Writers").

## Reading Rolodex

Instead of using a chart format, you may wish to encourage your students to create and file reading inventory cards either for all the selections they read or only for self-selected reading. On either 3x5 or 4x6 index cards, have them record basic information on the selection including title, author, and type of publication (book, magazine, newspaper, other), as well as a notation on whether they read all or only part of the selection (e.g., only one chapter or a particular article). On the reverse side, students should record briefly who or what the selection is about, along with a brief response to the questions, "Who do you think would like this reading selection? Why? Would you recommend that it be included in a classroom/school favorites list? Why or why not? To make the job of completing inventory cards easier for students, you may wish to preprint these headings on cardstock (see page 41 for template) or copy and paste the template onto index cards.

After students have accumulated several inventory cards, you may begin to explore with them (individually, in small groups, or as a class) any patterns or interesting findings they note. For example, you might consider whether students are making recommendations on a personal level or a more general level. Are they using gender-related language when they make recommendations? Are they making recommendations by connecting back to other reading selections, e.g., "if you liked _____, you would like this"?

Unlike more private reading logs, these file cards can be made available in a classroom file box that any student is welcome to consult. This resource creates opportunities for students to share the books they've read and helps create the conditions for more informal talk among peers about the books they read.

# READING CHOICES BINGO BOARD

| | | |
|---|---|---|
| **NON-FICTION**<br><br>_____<br>_____<br>_____<br><br>**by**<br>_____ | **FAIRYTALE/FOLKTALE**<br><br>_____<br>_____<br>_____<br><br>**by**<br>_____ | **HISTORICAL FICTION**<br><br>_____<br>_____<br>_____<br><br>**by**<br>_____ |
| **HUMOR**<br><br>_____<br>_____<br>_____<br><br>**by**<br>_____ | **FREE CHOICE**<br><br>_____<br>_____<br>_____<br><br>**by**<br>_____ | **MYSTERY**<br><br>_____<br>_____<br>_____<br><br>**by**<br>_____ |
| **FANTASY/SCI- FI**<br><br>_____<br>_____<br>_____<br><br>**by**<br>_____ | **BIOGRAPHY**<br><br>_____<br>_____<br>_____<br><br>**by**<br>_____ | **REALISTIC FICTION**<br><br>_____<br>_____<br>_____<br><br>**by**<br>_____ |

# FILE CARD READING INVENTORY

Title

Author

Type of selection

❑ book       ❑ entire selection

❑ magazine     ❑ part of the selection

❑ newspaper    (e.g., chapter or article)

❑ other

Who or what is this selection about?

_____

_____

_____

_____

Who would like this reading selection, and why? Would you
recommend that it be included in a favorites list? Why or why not?

## "Log" On Again

If students regularly keep a reading journal or log, have them go back and, for each reading selection referred to, note the gender of author(s) and main character(s), and then explain whether they think that male, female, or both male and female readers would like that selection and why. Depending on the format of their reading logs, students may add this information as completed entries or attach "post-it" notes with this analysis wherever they've recorded responses to different selections.

Use this information to initiate a discussion of the characteristics of books that lead students to believe the selections are intended for boys, for girls, or for both. Ask students to reflect on the choices they make as independent readers, to see if they seem to limit those choices to "boys' books" or "girls' books."

## Piggybacking on Popularity

You may find it possible to capitalize on an author's popularity to guide some of your students toward books with less typical protagonists—specifically, to guide some of the boys you teach toward novels with female protagonists or more nontraditional male protagonists. Our examination of a series of summer reading lists prepared by intermediate and middle school students to guide their peers' self- selected vacation-time reading revealed that some of the most consistently popular authors are Lloyd Alexander, Jerry Spinelli, and Chris Crutcher. In addition to their more familiar works, each has written at least one novel with a nontraditional protagonist, which you might recommend:

- Several Lloyd Alexander novels, including *Illyrian Adventure, El Dorado Adventure, Drackenberg Adventure, Jedera Adventure*, and *Philadelphia Adventure*, feature as protagonist Vesper Holly, a female Indiana-Jones–type character.

- From the pen of Jerry Spinelli, author of such popular novels as *Maniac Magee* and *Crash* comes *Wringer*, a book about a young boy who stands up for himself and rejects a damaging rite of passage for boys in his community.

- In *Staying Fat for Sarah Byrnes*, sports novel writer Chris Crutcher (*Stotan!, Athletic Shorts, Running Loose*) portrays the friendship between two outsiders—the fattest boy in school and a girl who had been disfigured by fire in early childhood. While a sports venue is again spotlighted (this time, the swimming pool), this novel sheds light as well on how we see ourselves and how others see us.

# 4

# READING ACROSS PURPOSES

There are many reasons for examining the availability of informational and functional texts, as well as literary selections, in the classroom and school library. As Myra Barrs notes, "Girls' generally higher levels of achievement in reading may reflect the nature of the reading demands made of them, and may in fact mask substantial under-achievement in some areas of reading that, for a complex of reasons, are less carefully monitored in schools, such as the reading of informational texts" (1993, p. 3).

Without teachers probing more deeply, girls' greater general proficiency in reading may obscure more uneven levels of performance when interacting with expository texts—precisely the kinds of texts that "count most" at the secondary level and beyond. Conversely, while many of the newest generation of reading texts and tests include at least some selections besides literary ones, boys—who often demonstrate a preference for, and greater facility constructing meaning from, informational selections—don't have sufficient opportunities to build upon those strengths and preferences in an everyday classroom context.

Increasingly, in response to new reading frameworks, teachers are thinking beyond narrative and are addressing a variety of genres and purposes for reading. Only recently, however, have publishers demonstrated awareness of this trend by providing reading selections that give students an opportunity to read related materials across purposes. Notable are Steck-Vaughan's *Pair-It Books*, which link leveled literary and informative texts, and such periodicals as *Ranger Rick*, *Appleseeds*, *Cobblestone*, and *Odyssey*, that offer themed issues containing not only informative articles, but also related activities, stories and poems. An Alfred A. Knopf imprint, Dragonfly Books™, has also taken the lead in formatting paperback editions of a number of children's titles with related informative selections and one or more activities inside the front and back covers.

Another positive development is the publication of more resources for the teaching of the reading and writing of nonfiction (see, for example, *Nonfiction Matters*, Harvey, 1998, and *Nonfiction Craft Lessons,* Portalupi & Fletcher, 2001). For a number of years, *Language Arts* has published a review, distinct from the year's notable children's books, of "outstanding nonfiction choices" for that year. Still, as the editors of *English Journal* (2001) recently noted:

> When we compare the number of fictional works we use in our courses against the number of nonfiction pieces we teach, we usually find that nonfiction comes out on

the short end. Though many of our students enjoy reading nonfiction for pleasure, for some reason we don't give it much attention in the English class.

Because high-quality informational and functional resources are still limited in number and topic, it falls to teachers to guide students to books of interest across purposes for reading.

# RECOMMENDING READING CLUSTERS

Once students' individual reading preferences have been identified, you may find it useful to share "book clusters"—sets of selections that share a common characteristic that may interest students (a particular topic or setting, for example), but that cut across purposes for reading. Consider the following scenarios:

◆ Jason has been enthralled by dinosaurs since preschool and can name them by the dozens and provide innumerable facts about prehistoric life. He is the first to pick up on the newest encyclopedic volume on dinosaurs, and Jason loved *Dinosaur Discovery* by Daniel Cohen. Its layout is familiar, with each creature accorded its pair of pages complete with a carefully done drawing and a fact-rich text. To Jason, you might recommend a delightful literary selection titled *Bone Poems*. Written by Jeff Moss, in consultation with curators at New York's Museum of Natural History, this volume contains tongue-in-cheek verses about an array of dinosaurs. What makes these poems unusual is the abundance of information embedded within them—there is a great deal the author needed to know about dinosaurs to compose these poems. Although Jason will have to wait a good many years to become a practicing paleontologist, he might enjoy using scissor and brush instead of trowel, as he reads directions in *Crafts for Kids Who Are Wild About Dinosaurs* (Kathy Ross).

◆ Jason's classmate, Nita, has always loved poetry. One of her favorite poets is David Florian, whose volumes introduce readers to all sorts of birds and beasts. She read his *Insectlopedia* and loved it, and was introduced to another volume of insect poems, Fleishman's *Joyful Noise: Poems for Two Voices*, in which each poem is structured as a dialogue between butterflies, bees, and other bugs. This is an ideal time to share with Nita a book like *Insects Are My Life*, by Megan McDonald. The intrepid main character is a young girl with a passion for insects, which she pursues in spite of classmates' teasing. Nita's budding exploration of the facts behind the fantastic can be supplemented with an audience-friendly informational book about insects (like David Suzuki's *Looking at Insects*) while her artistic bent might be encouraged by sharing *Crafts for Kids Who Are Wild about Insects* (Kathy Ross). The intersection between science and art provide common ground for both Nita and Jason, as they expand their competence in reading across all purposes through clustering of texts.

Some other suggested "clusters:"

## Clusters for Grades 3–5

- *What Is an Amphibian?* (Robert Sneddon)—Reading to be Informed
- *The Salamander Room* (Anne Mazer)—Reading for Literary Experience
- *Crafts for Kids Who Are Wild about Reptiles* (Kathy Ross)—Reading to Perform a Task

- *One Big Family: Sharing life in an African Village* (Ifeoma Onyefulu)—Reading to be Informed
- *A Kente Dress for Kenya* (Juwanda Ford)—Reading for Literary Experience
- *Ebele's Favourite: A Book of African Games* (Ifeoma Onyefulu)—Reading to Perform a Task

- *If You Lived in Colonial Times* (Anne McGovern)—Reading to be Informed
- *The Courage of Sarah Noble* (Alice Dalgliesh)—Reading for Literary Experience
- *Colonial Kids* (Laurie Carlson)—Reading to Perform a Task

- *Knights & Castles* (Kids Discover Magazine)—Reading to be Informed
- *A Door in the Wall* (Marguerite De Angeli)—Reading for Literary Experience
- *Days of Knights and Damsels: An Activity Guide* (Laurie Carlson)—Reading to Perform a Task

## Clusters for Grades 6–8

- *The Greek News* (Anton Powell & Philip Steele)—Reading to be Informed
- *Dateline: Troy* (Paul Fleischman)—Reading for Literary Experience
- *Spend the Day in Ancient Greece* (Linda Honan)—Reading to Perform a Task

- *The Long Road to Gettysburg* (Jim Murphy)—Reading to be Informed
- *Girl in Blue* (Ann Rinaldi)—Reading for Literary Experience
- *Civil War Days* (David King)—Reading to Perform a Task

- *Storm Warriors* (Elisa Carbone)—Reading to be Informed
- *The Cay* (Theodore Taylor)—Reading for Literary Experience
- *How the Weather Works* (Michael Allaby)—Reading to Perform a Task

- *Profiles of Great Black Americans: Female Leaders* (Richard Rennert)—Reading to be Informed
- *The Watsons Go to Birmingham* (Christopher Curtis)—Reading for Literary Experience
- *The Civil Rights Movement for Kids: A History with 21 Activities* (Mary Turck)—Reading to Perform a Task

# 5

# VALIDATING THE NEGATIVE

How many times have children heard the injunction, "If you don't have anything nice to say, don't say anything"? The underlying social convention seems to find its way into classroom "book talk," which almost invariably demands—explicitly or implicitly—a favorable stance towards the text. This expectation that students' evaluations of text will be complimentary is reinforced by teachers' familiarity with publishers' catalogues and lists of "best bets" and recommended titles.

When responding to text, however, boys are far more likely than girls to be critical and to say "No" when asked whether they would recommend a particular selection to a friend or classmate. Unfortunately, they frequently support that negative position only with such general statements as "because it was dumb" or "because it was babyish," rather than using specific details and examples from the text to develop their response. Girls are more likely to incorporate text references to support their viewpoint. However, they rarely express a negative position and often silence their dislike of a character, topic, or text as a whole. Both boys and girls can benefit, therefore, from activities that help to legitimize a negative stance towards text and provide them with ways of supporting that stance.

The following activity, "Rave Reviews and Book 'Boo's'," helps all students to incorporate explicit text support when responding to reading selections either positively or negatively and provides students with the vocabulary to talk about text in a variety of ways. The activity helps to validate negative responses and to demonstrate that a negative response can be developed with text support and precise language as fully and effectively as a positive response.

## RAVE REVIEWS AND BOOK "BOO'S"

**HOW TO GET READY:** duplicate "Rave Review/Book 'Boo'" Form (see page 48); have on hand highlighting markers.

**SUGGESTED GROUPING:** individual; share with small or whole group.

HOW TO INTRODUCE THE ACTIVITY(SAY/DO): "Often after we've read a book, others want to know our opinion of it. Did we like it or not? Why? Would we recommend it to them? For what reasons?"

# RAVE REVIEW/BOOK "BOO" FORM

Name _____

| Rave Review | Book "Boo" |
| --- | --- |
| | |
| | |
| | |
| | |
| | |
| | |
| | |
| | |
| | |
| | |
| | |
| | |
| | |
| | |
| | |

Elicit from students that readers' reasons for liking or disliking a book may include the plausibility or appeal of characters, the credibility of the plot, the length and pace of the book, perceptions regarding the accuracy and relevance of information, and the book's relationship to others on the same topic or by the same author.

"Sometimes, different readers will have opposite reactions to the same book." (Share an example of a positive and negative review such as the sample "Butterflies and Moths" in Figure 5.1.)

| Rave Review | Book "Boo" |
|---|---|
| I really liked the book "Butterflies and Moths" by David Carter. There was more about butterflies than moths in it, and I like butterflies and pretty moths. The real pretty moths live in other countries but the monarch butterfly lives in America. If you're interested in butterflies and moths, but especially butterflies, then this is the book for you. | I really didn't like the book "Butterflies and Moths" by David Carter. There was more about butterflies than moths in it, but I like moths and weird butterflies more than pretty insects like the monarch butterfly. I wish there was more information on strange ones like the death's head moth. Unless you're interested in butterflies more than moths, I don't think this is a book you'd like much either. |

*Figure 5.1 Sample Rave Review/Book "Boo"*

"Pick a book that you read recently and, using the form I distributed, write a review to describe the book and explain why you did or did not like it. Support your opinion with information and examples from what you read. If you liked the book and think others would too, record your review in the Rave Review column. If you did not like the book or think others would not, record your review in the Book 'Boo' column."

HOW TO DO THE ACTIVITY: Students may write their book reviews during or outside of class. After the reviews have been written, students will exchange their reviews with a peer or share them with a small group. To help students both as readers and writers understand what constitutes text support, students should highlight in their peer's review all the text-based ideas/information that support that reviewer's position. A minute to "hold up highlights" (raise highlighted papers so all classmates can see evidence of no/little/some/much text support) may follow, with students sharing examples (see Figure 5.2 for sample) of both Rave Reviews and Book "Boo's."

| Rave Review | Book "Boo" |
|---|---|
| I liked the book the house of dies drear. Thomas was a boy of many advantages. Thomas wouldn't take ~~know~~ no for a answer. Thomas was always looking for something that's up for grabes. I also say that because the book was ~~x~~ kind of funny. Thomas ~~xx~~ was having case of ~~x~~ Deja-vu the dream he had a dream of a foster he was running thought then ~~they~~ Thomas really was running the woods. | |

*Figure 5.2 The same book elicits a Rave Review (this page) and a Book "Boo" (page 51) from two different students.*

**Name** _____

| **Rave Review** | **Book "Boo"** |
|---|---|
| | I did not really like the house of dies drear because it talked too much about Thomas and not really show his relation to his father or twin brother well. I also did not like it because I did not really understand. At times the mystery was just confusing. It also did not make sense because Mr. Pluto was like a caretaker but also like a guard. |

Since much "book talk" (whether written by children or adults) to which students are exposed is positive, you will find it helpful to share some examples of published reviews that reflect an ambivalent or downright negative perspective. One excellent source of reviews that are more balanced—identifying weaknesses as well as strengths—is the *School Library Journal*. Using overheads or copies, have students highlight words and phrases that effectively convey a more mixed or even negative perspective (see Figure 5.3).

APPLEGATE, Stan. Natchez *Under-the-Hill*. Illus. By James Watling. 186p. maps. Notes. CIP. Peachtree. 1999. Pap. $8.95. ISBN 1-56145-191-6. LC 98-43051.

Gr 5-8-In this sequel to *The Devil's Highway* (Peachtree, 1998), Zeb, 14, encounters horse thieves and other outlaws as he travels the dangerous Natchez Trace in 1811 in search of his grandfather. Unfortunately, the adventure falls flat despite the presence of strong-willed, conscientious Zeb. The story's shortcomings lie in its inability to maintain a heightened sense of excitement due to one-dimensional supporting characters who appear haphazardly throughout and unclear motivations. Applegate does provide some historical facts about events in the book in an author's note and weaves a well-written, accurate depiction of Indian life in the early 1800s into the narrative. Though the ending is rushed and the escape of the horse thieves predictable, the various plot lines do come together. Fans of the first book will come away satisfied.

*Figure 5.3 One reviewer's language choices highlights a book's shortcomings.*
Reproduced with permission from School Library Journal © by Cahners Business Information, a division of Reed Elsevier Inc. For subscription information e-mail hchecinski@cahners.com.

To expand their ability to respond to texts either positively or negatively, you might have students identify pairs of antonyms for various words and phrases typically used when evaluating text. For example:

| + WORDS AND PHRASES | - WORDS AND PHRASES |
|---|---|
| happily, fortunately | unfortunately |
| is sustained, maintained, consistent | falls flat |
| strengths, highlights | shortcomings |
| ability, capacity | inability |
| complex, multidimensional, rich | one-dimensional |
| clear | unclear |
| well-paced | rushed/sluggish |
| unpredictable, surprising, suspenseful | predictable |

You may wish to reintroduce this activity periodically, to help students continue to expand the language they have for talking about text. You may also wish to call attention to review language that "damns with faint praise," often through subordination (e.g., while, though, although, lest, provided, unless, until, whenever). For example:

> Although the narrative tends to be long-winded, it nevertheless makes an effective read-aloud.

> While these titles introduce important themes such as the need to stand up to injustice and to seek positive change, they are marred by poor writing and amateurish artwork.

> Provided readers aren't expecting new facts, this is a useful compendium for the classroom.

Students will come to recognize that conjoining positive remarks and negative ones often creates an effect that is not balanced, but tips towards the negative.

## VARIATIONS/EXTENSIONS: SOME SUGGESTIONS

♦ With exposure to less-than-favorable as well as favorable reviews, students will become more sensitive to the notion of differing perspectives, and may be ready to entertain alternative perspectives. If so, you may wish to have students pick a book they liked, and write a Rave Review. Then, ask them to think about reasons why someone else might not like that book. Direct them to put themselves in that real or imaginary person's shoes, and write a Book "Boo." Alternatively, if they did not like a book, they should first write the Book "Boo" and then think about why someone else might actually like that book. Then, they should write a Rave Review as if they were that person (see Figure 5.4).

♦ After the whole class has read the same selection, have students decide if, overall, they'd give that selection a Rave Review or Book "Boo." Joining others of like opinion, they should brainstorm the merits and flaws of that selection (in terms of such features as characters, setting, illustrations, interest, audience appropriateness, etc.). Mirroring the game-show format of the popular "Family Feud," select a subgroup for each "family" (the "Raves" and the "Boo's"). As the rest of the students listen as judges, ask a series of questions to which students can respond positively or negatively. Suggested questions include:

• Would middle school students (__ grade students) find the main character realistic? Support your answer based on what you read and your own ideas.

• Did you find the ending of the story satisfying and/or believable? Support your answer based on what you read and your own ideas.

• Did you find the setting of the story well-established and purposeful? Support your answer based on what you read.

| **Rave Review** | **Book "Boo"** |
|---|---|
| I really liked the book Armageddon Summer by Jane Yolen and Bruce Coville. It makes itself out to be a science fiction fantasy novel by its flashy cover and its plot, through much of which the characters are working on preparations for the End of the World, and it also shows conflicting beliefs between the two people telling the story, as to wether the end would actually come or not. The inside view of the extreme religious cult through the eyes of two teenagers is thoroughly interesting, and I would recommend this book to anyone. | I read the novel Armagedden Summer and I just kept wishing for the end to come. When I first saw the book in the store, I was hypnotized by the many spinning colors of the flames and the angel wings on the cover, so I bought it in expectation of a great and wonderous science fiction fantasy with big world-crushing explosins and angels, or SOME-THING...but NO! NOTHING!! NOOOTHII/I NGG!!! Get my drift? As for our cult believer, character Merina, she needs to smack her psycho mom upside the head a couple times. |

*Figure 5.4 A middle school student looks at a novel from both sides and writes both a positive and a negative review.*

- Did chapter titles help to pique your interest, help move the story along, or help you understand what that part of the selection would be about? Support your answer based on what you read.

The first contestant on either team who can respond with text-based support—confirmed by the panel of judges who also read the book—wins a point for his or her team. At the end of a predetermined period of time, the team with the most points wins. Before the clock is reset and new "families" are selected, students should be permitted to change their minds about their overall positions regarding the selection and may switch teams.

♦ Sometimes we can give a book we've read a simple "thumbs up" or a "thumbs down" (a Rave or "Boo"). Often, however, a book provokes mixed reactions. We may enjoy and admire certain aspects of a book while finding other elements dissatisfying. After working with students to identify language for both positive and negative evaluations, you can encourage students—especially middle schoolers and more proficient intermediate students—to write reviews that convey more measured and nuanced perspectives. Doing this gives students an opportunity to consider ways to emphasize some claims and subordinate others. In the process, encourage students to reflect on the questions, "How can I admit a flaw, yet create a generally positive review? And, how can I acknowledge a book's strengths and yet give it a 'boo'?" A return to *Butterflies and Moths* (p. 49) provides an example of each:

  - Basically positive: Although somewhat narrow in its focus on a few familiar species, the book includes accurate and engaging information and vivid illustrations.

  - Basically negative: Despite the accuracy of the descriptions and illustrations in this book, the focus on only the most familiar species means this book rarely goes beyond common knowledge and offers little to someone already interested in the topic.

♦ Unlike many other kinds of writing that your students produce, book reviews have a real audience and many ready venues for publication. Amazon.com and other online booksellers welcome student written reviews, and many students have already seen their judgments about books—both positive and negative—literally broadcast across the globe. You can also submit student reviews electronically to such print publications as Scholastic's *Storyworks* (e-mail reviews to storyworks@scholastic.com) and Cobblestone Publishing's six magazines (www.cobblestonepub.com/KidsSubmit.html).

# Reality Check

Colleen wanted to see if it was true that the boys in her class tended to respond to text negatively more often than girls did, and if so, whether their responses indeed contained fewer specific details and examples to support their judgments. These are some of the reviews she received from her students:

♦ "I recently read a book the *Upstairs Room* by Johanna Reiss. It was not real good at all. The story is about a girl named Annie that has to hide in an attic from the German soldiers. If you want to know more read the book."

♦ "My last book, *Doll House Murders*, was about a 12 year old girl that has a mentally retarded sister that she has to take care of all the time. The 12 year old's name is Gomer and the other is Ellen. I didn't like this book because it was rushed."

♦ "Rowling, J.K. *Harry Potter and the Prisoner of Azkaban*, 435 pgs. In this sequel to *Harry Potter and the Chamber of Secrets*, Harry, 13, is once again at the wizarding school, Hogwarts, trying to keep up and stay out of trouble. After the recent escape of Sirius Black, a former prisoner at a wizard jail, certain precautions must be taken to ensure Harry's safety. With the help of his dead father's invisibility cloak, the Gamekeeper's hippogriff, and his friends, Harry solves the mystery of the prisoner of Azkaban in this fast-paced, exciting tale."

♦ "I have recently read the book, *Silent Storm*, by Sherry Garland. This book was about a 13-year-old girl Alissa who lived in a small house by the ocean with her grandfather in Maryland. She goes on many adventures with her friend Ty. Alissa cannot talk. She hasn't spoken since she was five because her mother died and her father left and she said she wouldn't talk to anyone until he came back. This book is very interesting and has a great ending."

♦ "*Number the Stars* was stupid. It was boring and it didn't give good information. It just was not good. The characters were Ellen."

♦ "The book *Crash* by Jerry Spinnelli is a very good book. I never wanted to put it down. The main character of the book is a kid known as Crash who is 13. He has a sister who is a nature freak, she really likes nature. There's a mall being built and his sister is against it. If you want to see if the mall is built read this book."

Can you determine the gender of each writer? What characteristics are leading to these conclusions? Check the key (upside down) to see if your predictions were correct. Where are opportunities for more extension and expansion of ideas, whether positive or negative?

key: boy, boy, girl, girl, boy, boy

# 6

# BECOMING MAPMAKERS OF A NEW WORLD: RETHINKING STORY AND CHARACTER MAPS

Our research into the performance of boys and girls as readers revealed that girls were more likely to consider the traits and actions of supporting or "peripheral" characters, while boys were more likely to concentrate their attention on a single, usually male, protagonist. One particularly striking finding was that boys often disregard female characters, writing them out of the story in its retelling. This is problematic not only because this "erasure" may mirror emerging gender stereotypes, but also—more immediately—because it may cause boys' readings to appear limited or even inaccurate.

For many boys, this treatment of character is coupled with a tendency to focus on the literal and more material problems in the stories they read, and on elements of action and plot. When reading the same selection, girls are more likely to focus on relational themes and implications. Boys' more limited focus, in turn, contributes to their generally poorer showing in classroom activities and on standardized assessments of reading.

The next set of activities is designed to help children think in new and more complex ways about story elements in general, and ways of describing characters in particular. These activities enable children to expand their perspectives to include secondary as well as primary characters and to widen their analyses of what stories "are about" by attending to how characters feel and how they change in response to "what happens." Mapping and remapping a literary selection is one useful way for students to consider the text from multiple perspectives.

## MAPPING AND REMAPPING

HOW TO GET READY: Select a narrative with which your class is familiar that features a male protagonist as well as multiple subsidiary characters of both genders. Ideally, it will be a story that offers both plenty of action and considerable opportunity to reflect on characters' motives and responses. Some possibilities include:

- *Uncle Willie and the Soup Kitchen,* Karen DiSalvo-Ryan

- *The Watsons go to Birmingham*, Christopher Paul Curtis

- Any of Phillip Pullman's trilogy, *The Golden Compass, The Subtle Knife, The Amber Spyglass*

If students are familiar with, and have used a traditional story map before (see p. 59 for one example), have them work individually or in small groups to map the selection you have cho-

---

# Killing Kids With Kindness?

The past decade or so has witnessed frequent use of graphic organizers (also called cognitive maps, critical thinking maps, or story maps, among other terms) as a learning strategy. These tools for visualizing key ideas and information have been promoted particularly for students with learning disabilities and for struggling or less-skilled readers and writers. The more such forms proliferate, the more a potentially useful tool for students to recall and reflect upon their reading and make some strategic choices when planning their writing, is being misused.

Graphic organizers ought not become this generation's worksheets or dittos, for which the "name of the game" is filling out the form. Nor should visual appeal distort or limit students' desire to redirect or reshape an understanding, as it does when students feel they must force-fit a certain number of events (typically four or five) into a classic story map or story-elements graphic organizer. Typically, when organizers are comprised of boxes, cells, or shapes, students feel compelled to add as many ideas or details as cued for—and no more; alternatively, when organizers are designed to reflect a recognizable shape (a face, a human body, a table, for example), students feel compelled to add "all the right parts," and in the right amounts.

Some excellent graphic organizers may be distorted by applying them to a process for which they were not intended—most frequently, by using an organizer that is highly effective as a framework that can be used before, during, and after reading, into one that is ineffective or even detrimental when applied to the planning of writing. No author we know of, for example, completes a story map first, on her way to planning a novel; no reporter blindly sequences information in the order of "who, what, when, where, how, and why" on a predetermined form. The beauty of planning and prewriting tools such as outlines, lists, and webs, is that they are flexible and evolving. Thinkers, readers and writers can find a "home" for any ideas, information, or details they believe important.

We prefer to use graphic organizers as a starting point for revising and reshaping thinking and learning. Typically, the activities in this chapter that utilize graphic organizers assume that students will be encouraged to add, remove, and change components if they wish to do so. Thus, we channel the assumptions students generally make when filling in forms and challenge them to become "mapmakers of a new world."

---

# TRADITIONAL STORY MAP

**Title** _____

**Setting**

_____

_____

_____

_____

**Characters**

_____  _____

_____  _____

_____  _____

_____  _____

**Problem**

_____

_____

_____

Event 1 _____

Event 2 _____

Event 3 _____

Event 4 _____

Event 5 _____

**Solution**

_____

_____

_____

sen. Any story element organizer that provides a visual framework in which to identify setting (which may be subdivided into time and place), characters, problem/goal, main events or action(s), and solution/outcome will do. If students are unfamiliar with a traditional story map graphic organizer, introduce one and guide students through its completion.

**SUGGESTED GROUPING:** small and whole group.

**HOW TO INTRODUCE THE ACTIVITY(SAY/DO):** "Sometimes, when we read a story or novel, we use a graphic organizer to help us gather important ideas and details, and to better understand the relationships among those ideas and details. Recently, we used a story map to help us recall important elements of _____ [identify particular story or novel]."

"Do you think all maps of the same story have to be the same?" (Elicit students' opinions and support.)

"Let's look at your story maps for a moment. Who are the characters in the story you read?" (Have students identify characters. If they have focused only on the main character, be sure to identify others, named and unnamed. Help students recognize that although some classmates may have omitted various characters, the selection they read included many characters, both major and supporting.)

"To help us reflect upon a particular character, we can use a different graphic organizer, one that helps us relate a character's key traits to particular actions and events in the story." (Distribute to each small group one copy of the character trait organizer on p. 61.)

Assign a character to each small group of students. Not all characters need to be assigned; however, be sure that male and female, major and supporting characters are represented. If students are analyzing a chapter book, they may choose to focus on a single chapter.

"As a group, take a few minutes to complete the character trait organizer for one of the characters in the story (novel) we've read." (Give groups sufficient time to complete the character trait map for their assigned character and then continue the discussion.)

"When we focus on character traits and actions or events that embody them, what understandings can we gain? What else might we want to know or better understand about this story that isn't made apparent when we focus on character traits?" (Elicit responses; be sure to guide students to recognize that a focus only on a given character's actions may ignore interplay between and among characters, the feelings and motivations that lie beneath what characters do, or how characters respond to events in which they are not directly involved but toward which they nevertheless have reactions.)

"There is clearly much more we can say about characters and events in this story than what we captured when we focused on character traits and key events. Therefore, your group will now reconvene to "remap" the story using a new organizer, an 'Action-Reaction Character Map.'" (Distribute copies of the "Action-Reaction Character Map" on page 62).

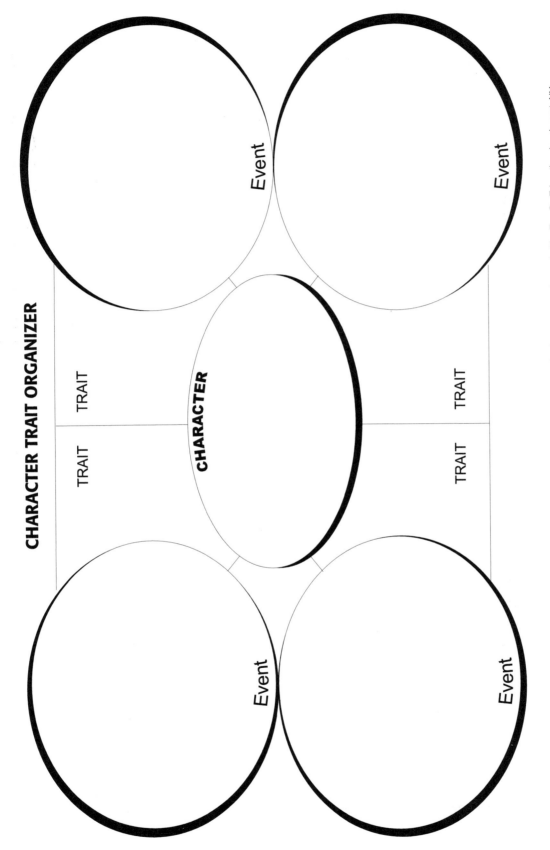

**CHARACTER TRAIT ORGANIZER**

Event

Event

TRAIT

TRAIT

**CHARACTER**

TRAIT

TRAIT

Event

Event

# ACTION-REACTION CHARACTER MAP

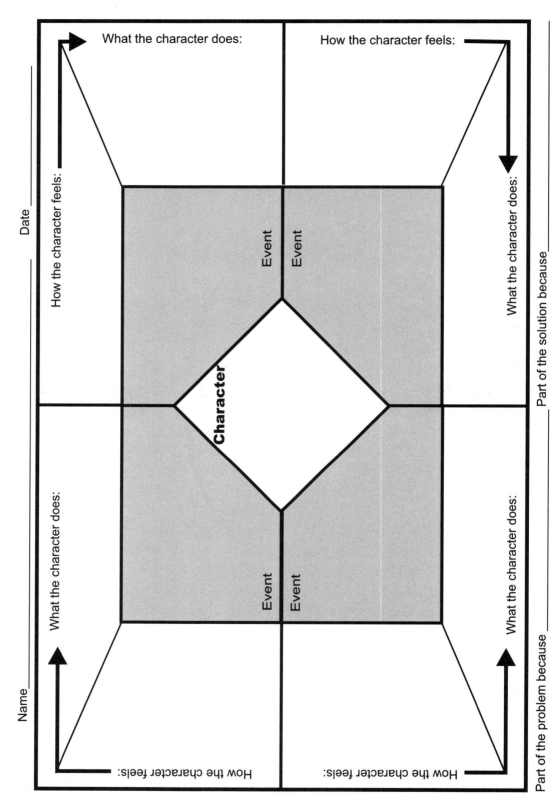

Name _____

Date _____

What the character does:

How the character feels:

How the character feels:

What the character does:

What the character does:

Event

Event

**Character**

Event

Event

What the character does:

How the character feels:

How the character feels:

Part of the problem because _____

Part of the solution because _____

"Think about and discuss as a group your assigned character's role in the story or chapter. Begin by recording the name of that assigned character in the center. Identify three or four key events in the story—these may or may not be the same events that you identified on the original story or character map. These events may have involved your character directly or only indirectly. Discuss and determine not only what, if any, part your character played in each event (what he or she did) but how that character felt about that event. After discussion, complete the remapping of this story from the perspective of the character assigned to your group."

**HOW TO DO THE ACTIVITY:** Groups may conduct discussion and complete the "Action-Reaction Character Map" concurrently or as an activity that takes place during guided reading with groups. After all groups have completed their maps, plan for sharing and discussion, perhaps first through exchange between groups and then with the whole class. Generate from the similarities and differences among students' maps the following ideas/ understandings:

◆ Different characters contribute to what happens in a story

◆ Those characters may have different perspectives about what happens and why

◆ Different characters may contribute in various ways to a conflict or main problem in a story

◆ Different characters may contribute in various ways to the solution in a story

Be sure at some point to return discussion to the impact of using the different graphic organizers as a way of mapping the story to gain understanding of characters and key events. Have students consider ways in which their perspectives or orientation toward the story changed. Which organizer might provide the best "blueprint" for summary or account of what the story "was about?" Why?

# VARIATIONS/EXTENSIONS

## Angles of Vision

Although the "Action-Reaction Character Map" can help students see stories and novels in new and more complex ways, it is not designed to highlight different characters' reactions to the same event. To elicit this "Rashomon-like" understanding, you may wish to introduce a modified map, "Angles of Vision" (page 64) that puts a single event at the center and directs students' attention to different characters' role in and reaction to that event.

## What's It About?

This next activity enables students to experiment with ordering story elements without the use of a "map" or organizer. Begin by asking students to complete the single sentence, "This story is about _____." Tally on the chalkboard or an overhead the number of students who include each of the elements taught to journalists—who, what, when, where, why and how (the 5 W's and 1 H). If students include more than one element, indicate the

# ANGLES OF VISION CHARACTER MAP

From *Reading, Writing, and Gender* by Goldberg and Roswell (©2002). Permission to duplicate for classroom use is granted by Eye On Education, Larchmont, NY.

Name _____

Date _____

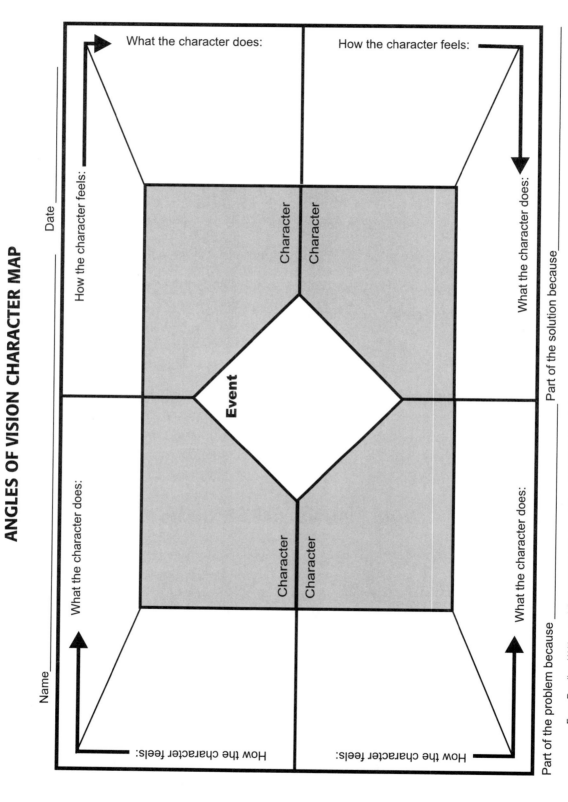

What the character does:

How the character feels:

How the character feels:

What the character does:

Character

Character

Event

Character

Character

What the character does:

How the character feels:

How the character feels:

What the character does:

Part of the problem because _____

Part of the solution because _____

order of the elements in parentheses. You are likely to find that the majority of students focus on character and plot (e.g., "This story is about a boy who…" "This story is about some girls who…"). You may find as well that girls are more likely than boys to present the "what" as an abstraction or emotion rather than as an action.

Give every student a sheet of paper on which the 5 W's and 1 H are written. Have them cut or tear the elements apart, so they'll each have six separate strips. Each student should then shuffle his or her strips, and reorder them without looking (Having a partner draw these strips or "straws" and putting a number on each, is a handy way to do this).

Each student will then summarize one of several selections the class has read, following the order of his or her set of strips. Ask students to reflect upon, and share ideas about, the effect that changing the order has upon the summary. Discuss/debate the order that gives the best idea of what the selection "is about." Students should recognize that there may be more or less effective ways to summarize, but that there is certainly more than one good way to do so.

Middle schoolers are ready to take an additional step and explore how context and purpose can determine the ordering of elements. Sometimes it is most important for a summary to call attention to theme or to a particular dilemma that unfolds in a book. You can help your students to see how different summary leads can direct an audience's attention to different elements by sharing examples such as the following:

| EMPHASIS | LEAD |
|---|---|
| A dilemma or conflict | A question (e.g., "What would you do if you knew a friend had broken the law?") |
| A current social issue | A striking fact or statistic; reference to a news item (e.g., A 15-year-old boy in South Africa has a 50 percent chance of contracting AIDS) |
| A unique perspective | A quotation (e.g., Martin Luther King once said, "If you go to the back of the bus, you belong at the back of the bus.") |

Additional "leads" might include a reference to another book, an anecdote, an analogy, an invitation to the reader to imagine a scenario, or an extended description of a place or object.

## Summaries and Story Maps

Across grade levels, students' ability to summarize a text is central to examining and extending meaning in other ways. One way to help students with summarizing skills is to demonstrate the relationship between summaries (which convey the gist of a story as a whole) and story maps (which graphically break apart key elements in a literary selection). To do so, we recommend you begin by having students independently write a summary of a story they've read.

Review these summaries on your own, to determine the extent to which you can differentiate them by student author's gender. You may wish, for example, to look for some of the differences our research uncovered. Did the student focus only on the actions of a main character? Did the student recount actions and emotions, or actions alone?

Your students' next step should be to complete a traditional story map and then use the information on that map to revisit their summaries. This process will help them both to flesh out their summaries with recollections about characters and to confirm or correct the accuracy of details about story events and the roles that various characters play in those events. You may wish to extend this process by having students complete an "Action-Reaction" and/or "Angles of Vision" character map before once again returning to, and possibly revising, their summaries. Finally, have students compare versions of their summaries and discuss the impact of widening their perspectives to consider the role of subsidiary characters. They are likely to experience a shift in the "center of gravity" so that their perception of stories becomes less linear and more complex.

As part of your efforts to help students summarize effectively, you may also want to increase their awareness of their response to story elements in summary reviews written by others. Have students write brief reviews of classroom library selections on a 3 x 5 card, which should be attached to the book cover when they return the book to its display location. When making subsequent selections, ask students to add their name beneath the reviewer's, on the card, and to highlight on the attached review the words or phrases (if any) that influenced their decision to select that book. Periodically initiate a conversation with your students (in small groups or as one unit) about what they notice about what's been highlighted. Are they drawn in by details about characters, setting, and plot? Are they drawn in by connections made to other titles or authors? Are they drawn in by the critical language of reviews (words like "exciting" or "interesting," and labels like "cliffhanger" or "tearjerker")? It is very likely that they will recognize the power of traditional story elements and summaries to engage others. Thus, this conversation will not only enhance students' thoughtful production and consumption of summaries and reviews, but will also support their sense of identity as members of a connected community of readers.

# 7

# BETWEEN THE TWO OF US—AUTHOR AND AUTHORITY: ENCOURAGING INTERPRETIVE READING

When boys are asked to retell a story they have heard or read, they are likely to focus on the literal and material problems of stories, on explicit components of plot and setting, and on informational elements. They like to name features, not explain them, and seem reluctant to go "further and deeper." Boys themselves explain that their impatience is fueled by the belief that if something has already been said or done (particularly if said or done well enough) there is little point to doing it again. It is they, rather than their female classmates, who are more likely to respond to assessment questions by asserting, "I already told you that," or "As I already said...." Thus, when we ask students to construct meaning, and in so doing, to position themselves as partners with an author, we may be creating an inherently discomfiting situation for some of the boys, who go to text typically to "find out" and not to "fill in." We may be able to induce more students, boys and girls alike, to read between the lines if we give them the sense that they have a separate, and expert, job to do—to collaborate with the author of a text as a translator, go-between, or "editor."

## EDITOR'S NOTES

HOW TO GET READY: Find a selection (literary or informative) that is either preceded or followed by a brief comment from someone other than the author. Many anthologized selections, as well as stories and articles in kid-friendly newspapers and magazines, are formatted this way. "Just for Kids," a weekly section in our local newspaper, the *Baltimore Sun*, provides one ideal resource.

SUGGESTED GROUPING: small group, whole group, then individual

**HOW TO INTRODUCE THE ACTIVITY (SAY/DO):** Find or create a set of five or six "Editor's Notes" to accompany various stories or articles with which your class is not likely to be familiar. For example:

- Extra-large amounts of courage can sometimes be found in extra-small packages (*A Brave Little Princess,* Beatrice Masini).

- Now all grown up, a famous trespasser tries to make amends (*Goldilocks Returns*, Lisa Campbell Ernst).

- A pair of pants causes a stir in society's attitude towards women (*You Forgot Your Skirt, Amelia Bloomer,* Shana Corey).

- Finicky eaters get their just desserts (*I Will Never Not Eat a Tomato,* Lauren Child).

Display your "Editor's Notes" without identifying the texts to which they refer on a chalkboard or flip chart.

"What could these statements possibly mean? What things do you know about, or have you read about or experienced, that support any of these statements?" (Have students share their ideas.)

"Each of these statements is an "Editor's Note" that precedes a particular story. Each statement has a job to do, but I'm not sure what that job is. Today, you'll be looking at some selections to help figure that out."

**HOW TO DO THE ACTIVITY:** Divide the class into groups and give each group one of the selections previewed in the "Editor's Notes." Instruct students to decide which "Editor's Note" matches their selection and to determine how they made that decision. Each group should prepare a brief list of "evidence" they find.

After students have shared and defended their match-ups, have students consider the function each "note" serves. Students should recognize after discussion that the "Editor's Notes" each function in a somewhat different way, for example, as a synopsis, snapshot, preview, overview, teaser, inside joke, or pun. Have students identify characteristics that distinguish the synopsis-type notes (those that tell in a global way what the selection is mainly about) from those that involve some sort of interpretation. In cases that involve interpretation, the editor has a voice that is distinct from the author's, and was doing his own, rather than the author's business.

Next, assign or have students select a brief story or article. After they have read it, have them prepare an "Editor's Note" that goes beyond synopsis, to give a unique perspective towards the text. Anthologies such as those published for the Junior Great Books program are an excellent source of selections crying out for such "Editor's Notes" to pique readers' interest and facilitate the anticipatory thinking that is part of proficient readers' "before reading" habits and strategies. Instead of assigning the same story to the entire class, you might have students work in pairs or small groups to read different selections and generate possible "Editor's

Notes" for each. These notes can be shared and compared, and ultimately used to create an "enhanced" table of contents for the anthology as a whole—something that can guide students' choices when reading stories from the anthology.

## VARIATIONS/EXTENSIONS: SOME SUGGESTIONS

♦ Invite your students to role-play different styles/voices for the Editor's Note. For example, they might be assigned the "tongue-in-cheek" note, or the "play-on-words" note, or the "idiomatic expression" note. As each note is shared, be sure to have other students react to it, determining what, if anything, it adds to their experience of the text itself.

♦ Establish a particular audience (and purpose) for whom a set of published or student-written selections might be intended. Have each student write an "Editor's Note" to a selection (other than their own, if these have been student-generated). Then, share selections and their companion notes, and discuss whether each note is appropriate to the given audience and purpose.

# 8

# EXPLORING MULTIPLE PERSPECTIVES

Both as readers, when adopting a personal stance to make reader-text connections, and as writers, when creating stories and informational texts, boys often demonstrate difficulty assuming perspectives different from their own or reflecting on the world around them from someone else's point of view. Girls display a greater willingness to "step into another person's shoes," but may not draw on a full range of information to convincingly convey what they know. When we invite students to step out into the world around them, as they do in the next activity, "Parallel Lives," they can use what they've learned as readers and writers to consider differences and commonalities among various peoples, places, periods of time, and of course, gender.

*Figure 8.1 The cover of* A Country Far Away *forecasts the book's comparative format.*

In this activity, students will use both prior knowledge and an informative selection about children in another land to create their own "mini-versions" of *A Country Far Away,* a picture book that introduces readers to the similarities and differences between their own lives and the lives of children from a rural African village (see Figure 8.1). The book is designed to encourage comparisons between two contemporary settings—a fairly urban western community and a rural African village. On each page, illustrations depicting these different settings, and the people within them, appear above and below a sentence or two that accompanies the picture panels and highlights the commonality of human experiences (e.g., "Today was an ordinary day. I stayed home," or "Today we went into town to do some shopping").

# PARALLEL LIVES

**HOW TO GET READY:** Prepare copies of the comparison form titled "In Another Country Far Away..." (page 73). Select several brief reading selections on children from other lands. Two excellent sources for such selections are *Children from Australia to Zimbabwe*, by Maya Ajmera and Anna Rhesa Versola and *Children Just Like Me*, by Anabel and Barnabas Kindersley.

**SUGGESTED GROUPING:** Whole class followed by small group and individual activity.

**HOW TO INTRODUCE THE ACTIVITY:** Read *A Country Far Away* by Nigel Gray aloud to your class. Instruct students to look carefully at the illustrations in this early reader's picture book as you read and note similarities and differences between the pictures of life in each community. Then, lead a discussion about these observations. You may wish to have students record similarities and differences (using a Venn Diagram) or differences only (using a T-chart) on the chalkboard or a flip chart.

**HOW TO DO THE ACTIVITY:** Assign students to small groups, each of which will read about and focus on children from a different country. You may wish to create heterogeneous groups, or, instead, to differentiate instruction by assigning texts of varying degrees of difficulty to each of a number of homogeneous reading groups. In the latter manner, all students, regardless of reading level, can be engaged in the same, meaningful work.

After reading and discussing their group's selection, students should each choose a different focus for a comparison between themselves (and/or other children from their community) and a child or children from the country they have read about. Students will draw upon information they have obtained from their readings and their own ideas, observations, and experiences, and will use words and pictures to communicate their comparison on the split-screen activity page (see Figure 8.2 on page 74). You may wish to have younger students focus on something that both children or groups of children have in common and record those ideas in writing in the central portion of the page, and then use the illustration panels to show differences with drawings and labels (as in the model, *A Country Far Away*). Older students should be encouraged to write about the common feature or features in the center portion and then to elaborate in writing alongside their picture panels. Elements of environment and culture that can be compared include, among many others:

- clothing
- schools
- homes
- transportation
- toys, games, favorite activities
- families
- religious observances
- community—physical and man-made features

If you wish, you may have each group bind their pages together to form a sequel to *A Country Far Away*. This "published" copy would make a wonderful gift to children in another classroom.

# IN ANOTHER COUNTRY FAR AWAY

Today, I wrote a letter to the leader of my country.

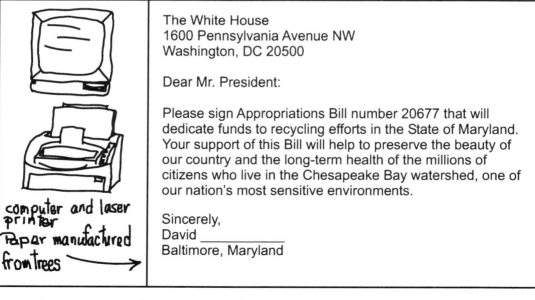

*Figure 8.2 A student compares letter-writing in ancient Egypt and today.*

# VARIATIONS/EXTENSIONS:
# SOME SUGGESTIONS

♦ Based on units of study in your curriculum, students might draw comparisons between the time in which they live and another period of time. You may wish to modify the manipulative to read "A Time Long Ago," or simply have students create their own "split-screen" form. Possible time periods might be ancient Greece or Rome, medieval times, or colonial times. Alternatively, you may wish to use this type of activity to explore more subtle similarities and differences among subgroups of a peoples (e.g., specific Native American tribes).

♦ You need not use *A Country Far Away* as a model to introduce "split-screen" thinking to help students reflect on other similarities and differences among cultures. The double picture panel form by itself is a helpful organizer for students to record ideas and information about cross-cultural comparisons based on topics such as jobs, tools, homes, schools, celebrations, and family.

♦ Students can use "split-screens" to compare the lives, experiences, and interests of boys and girls in their own, or in another, culture. They might consider, for example, preferred games, toys, clothing, or friends.

# 9

# UNDERSTANDING THE FUNCTIONS OF TEXT FEATURES

When children are asked to respond to questions dealing with text features—the particular elements of style and format that authors use to help readers navigate through, and make meaning of, text—boys' and girls' proficiency appears to differ little, although their approaches to text may. Boys' relative strength when analyzing how meaning is made is very likely the result of their familiarity with texts—often informational—that are characterized by rich visual content and a conspicuous organizational plan. In fact, researchers from Great Britain (Barrs & Pidgeon, 1993; Millard, 1997) have repeatedly found that boys are much more inclined than girls to read informational texts such as topic-based magazines, how-to books, and statistical and factual synopses (e.g., sports stat sheets and almanacs). Such selections tend to be both visually appealing and purposeful—enabling boys to "cut to the chase" and find particular facts or details of interest.

You may wish to capitalize, therefore, on boys' comfort with, and willingness to, examine the relationship between text features and the making of meaning, by incorporating more of those types of activities into your reading instruction and linking them to opportunities to extend meaning and more effectively read "between the lines." Girls in your class will benefit from the opportunity to become more analytical about how texts are "put together" and about how to navigate through the kind of information-rich texts that become increasingly central in the curriculum after the middle school years.

Beginning with "How Meaning Is Made/What Meaning Is Made," the following activities invite students to look more closely at both informational and literary selections as artifacts and to explore the functions of a variety of text features that shape readers' making of meaning.

## HOW MEANING IS MADE/WHAT MEANING IS MADE

HOW TO GET READY: Pick a reading selection related to a topic you've been addressing in science or social studies that is rich in distinctive text features. These text features might include the purposeful use of different fonts, captions, headings, illustrations (drawings or photographs), diagrams, maps, graphs, and insets. Using a photocopy, cover up all these features so that what students first see consists only of the title and the print copy of the text.

Alternatively, you may wish to retype and copy for students only the title and text. Articles from student-oriented publications such as *Time for Kids* and *Storyworks* are particularly appropriate for this activity. We have used *Our Place in Space*, one of a series of family activity magazines produced by the Museum of Natural History, as a model in the "How to do the activity" section below.

SUGGESTED GROUPING: pairs, small and whole group

HOW TO INTRODUCE THE ACTIVITY(SAY/DO): "Over the past few [days, weeks], we've been learning about _____ (name your topic here; for example we would say "Space"). Today I would like to share with you a selection I found that tells us more about _____ (your topic). With a partner, read this selection. Highlight any ideas and information that you think is especially important or interesting to someone who wants to learn about _____ (your topic)."

Distribute photocopies of the edited selection, and give students sufficient time to read and respond to your directions. Then, elicit students' thoughts about the ideas and information that seemed especially important.

"How did you decide which ideas were most important or interesting? What clues, if any, are there to help you tell what is especially important?"

HOW TO DO THE ACTIVITY: Now distribute the original text (see Figure 9.1 for the example we used, "A Closer Look at Mars"). Ask students to reread and examine this selection. They should work in pairs to identify the differences between the edited version and the original, and to explain how the additional text features in the original contribute to their understanding of important ideas and information.

As a "next step," reflect with students on their responses. For example, one group of student said the following about the impact of text features on their understanding of the selection "A Closer Look at Mars":

"The different sized print for 'telescopes,' 'spacecraft' and 'robots' helped make clear that these are three major ways scientists have learned about Mars."

"The illustration on the side showed where Mars is in relation to the other planets in our solar system."

"The insert about Pluto highlighted that what our parents and grandparents thought about Pluto might not really be true."

"The photograph shows what a volcano on Mars looks like from a spacecraft. Wow!"

"The different colors of the boxes tells you that some of the information belongs together, and some doesn't."

"The cute, pot-bellied cartoon Martian made me think this section would be silly ideas or something fun for me to do."

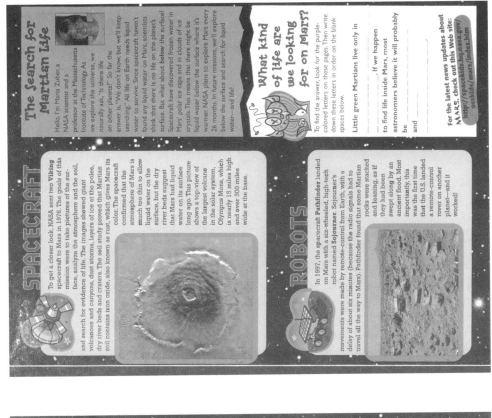

*Figure 9.1 "A Closer Look at Mars" from Our Place in Space: A Kid's Guide to the Universe.*

Text and illustrations © 2001 American Museum of Natural History, New York. Reprinted with permission. Also available in this magazine series: *Biodiversity: It Takes All Kinds to Make a World, Infection Detection Protection, Our Dynamic Planet,* and *The Gene Scene.* For information on how to order *Our Place in Space* or other magazines in this series, call 1-212-769-5993 or e-mail at center@amnh.org.

Based on the experience of other teachers, you may find that boys are likely to name and generalize about features (e.g., "The different colors of the boxes tell you that some of the information belongs together and some doesn't"), whereas girls are likely to give specific examples, often with personal connections (e.g., "The cute, pot-bellied cartoon Martian made me think this section would be silly ideas or something fun for me to do."). Take this opportunity to model the extension and expansion of observations about text features to make explicit the ways in which they contribute to readers' making of meaning.

## VARIATIONS/EXTENSIONS: SOME SUGGESTIONS

♦ This activity can be adapted for use with a literary selection infused with a variety of text features. Typically, children's literary selections include such text features as distinct or varied font (bold face, italicized, and/or differently-sized print), illustrations, vignettes (illustrated letters to lead off a paragraph or whole text), and borders. If considering the whole book as an artifact, look for meaning-bearing end-papers and appendices as well (some of our favorites are *Stella Luna, Sam Johnson and the Blue Ribbon Quilt*, and *A River Runs Wild*).

♦ Children's poetry provides abundant examples of the use of font and format to impact the making of meaning. David Florian (*beast feast, Insectlopedia, on the wing*), for example, uses horizontal, vertical, and diagonal spacing between letters and words to great effect; Jeff Moss (*Bone Poems*) likes to play with italics and capital letters; Jack Prelutsky (*A Pizza the Size of the Sun, The New Kid on the Block, Something Big Has Been Here*) utilizes all sorts of font sizes and intensity, as well as placement of text in shaped poems; and Paul Fleischman's "poems for two voices" in *Joyful Noise* depend on their columnar format and the space between stanzas to signal monologue, dialogue, and choral reading. Examination and appreciation of the construction of these works add a dimension to the reading of poetry especially welcomed by boys who may not, under other circumstances, choose to read poems.

♦ In many educational communities, a distinction is made between texts intended to provide information and those that provide directions on how to do or make something. Readers, both children and adults alike, typically ask themselves various questions when they read directions in anticipation of doing or making something. For example, they may ask, "Based on what I read...

- do I have available everything I need to do this?"
- do I have the time to do this?"
- do I have the skills to do this?"
- can I do this alone or will I need help?"
- will following these directions lead to the result I want?"
- in what order do I complete these steps? What do I do first, next, after that?"

Text features play a significant role in guiding readers in the construction of meaning when readers are engaged in functional reading, and these features help readers answer questions such as these. For example, directions and other "how-to" texts often include meaning-bearing variations in font, bullets or numbers, captions and headings, many types of insets, and illustrations used for a wide array of purposes (e.g., to help visualize particular steps in a process, the finished product, or uses for the finished product).

Consequently, our judgments about the clarity and effectiveness of such selections are based on the meaningful use of text features ("Did the illustrations help me to understand where the parts go? Were any special warnings or possible problems made clear?"). Explicit references to text features and their specific effects will help boys and girls alike make connections between formal aspects of text and ways those aspects contribute to the construction of meaning when reading.

♦ You may find it useful to display in your classroom a chart illustrating the most frequently encountered text features (see page 82). Alternatively, you may wish to collaborate with students in constructing a text feature bulletin board display. Post headings with the most commonly used text features, and invite students to find examples of these in self-selected readings. Copy and arrange under each heading those student-selected examples, frequently adding and changing the examples to maintain interest. You may wish to refer to this display as part of instruction in previewing reading selections to establish purpose for reading—how does the text signal that the author intended it to be read primarily for literary experience, to be informed, or to perform a task?

♦ Reading/Writing Connection: Often when we create a text, we make use of visual elements to signal to readers the importance of certain ideas, the order of ideas, or the relationships among ideas. Sometimes, however, we must rely on signaling words to do so. Similarly, as readers, when visual clues are absent we must attend to those signaling words to fully understand a text. To help students understand this analogous relationship and to transfer its implications from reading texts to writing, have them return to the "text feature chart." For each feature (boldface, italics, numbering, bullets, boxes, etc.), ask students to list words that can fulfill the same function.

For example:

| | |
|---|---|
| ♦ Bold | *most important, the point is…* |
| ♦ Numbering | *first, second, next, finally…* |
| ♦ Boxes | *in contrast, an interesting example is, one story that illustrates this point…* |
| ♦ Larger font | *especially, in particular, extremely* |
| ♦ Italics | *that is, in other words, you might say* |

# TEXT FEATURES USED BY AUTHORS

Colors

Maps

☐ **BOXES**

PHOTOGRAPHS

Bullets/Steps

●     1.
◆     2.
      3.

_Underlining_

**Bold** print

Captions

Arrows ← ◀

This is a square.
It has 4 equal sides.

**BIG** letters

 Graphs

← Stem

*Pronunciation Key*
ear (e$\tilde{r}$)

Labels

*Italic* print

 **DIAGRAMS**

Ask students to pick a visually rich, two-page excerpt from an informational book on a topic of interest to them. *Eyewitness Books* (DK Publishing) provide a variety of texts of this sort on many different topics. In pairs, have students plan how they would order and connect the information from this text into a single, print-only version. Then, have student share these plans with the class as a group. Since the purpose of this activity is to develop students' understanding of the verbal equivalents of visual elements, they need not ever actually compose the extended text for this activity to be meaningful.

# 10

# LINKING READING IN THE CONTENT AREAS TO PERSONAL AND PRIOR KNOWLEDGE

It is easy to overlook the content areas of mathematics, science, and social studies when our attention is focused on patterns of performance by boys and girls as readers and writers. Content area scores from various state and national assessments, for example, rarely cause a "caution light" to go on, because it appears by most measures that boys and girls are not performing at significantly different levels of proficiency in these areas. The similarity between boys' and girls' overall performance in mathematics, science, and social studies, however, masks important differences in their ability to respond to particular kinds of questions. Text-dependent activities, those that require that students wear their readers' and writers' hats as well as those of a given content area, often reveal the same gap in performance that we see in traditional English language arts activities.

Most text-based instructional and assessment activities in the content areas require little more than information location and retrieval. Students read a selection or passage, and subsequently must respond to questions (like the ubiquitous "end of chapter" questions that characterize many middle school content area textbooks) about the ideas and information contained therein. Boys and girls do not appear to respond differently to these sorts of activities. However, this is not the case when responding to "double- or triple-barreled" questions. Such questions require students to apply text-based and prior knowledge about one or more content areas (whether drawn from personal experience and observation or as the result of instruction) to solve a problem or explain a phenomenon. These more complex questions typically take the form: "Use A and B to explain how Y shows Z." In these instances, boys are far more likely than girls to attend to only one component of these complex and multilayered questions—typcally, the one that they perceive as the "point" of the question.

The following activity, "Part to Whole," is intended to help students—boys in particular—to become more proficient at "unpacking" complex questions to ensure that they address them fully and well.

# PART TO WHOLE

**HOW TO GET READY:** Pick a set of directions for making a model or conducting a science investigation that models an observable phenomenon. Craft a question that uses the following frame:

Explain how _____ (the title of the selection) is a model of _____ (thing or phenomenon) that you can observe in everyday life/in the world around you (pick one).

To illustrate the use of this frame and an example of its application, we have used a selection titled "More or Less" from Janice VanCleave's *Earth Science for Every Kid* (1991) (see Figure 10.1).

**SUGGESTED GROUPING:** large group

**HOW TO INTRODUCE THE ACTIVITY (SAY/DO):** "We've learned that sometimes scientists use models to better understand the world around them. They may use a model to show something that is too big (the earth), too small (a mosquito), too fast (a chemical reaction), too slow (erosion), or too dangerous (a volcano) to study it otherwise. They may use a model to represent something that we might only see under certain conditions."

Distribute copies of the selection.

"These directions describe how to do an activity that models something. Read the directions, and then, in your notebook [science journal, reading log] respond to the following question: 'Explain how the investigation "More or Less" is a model of a condition that you can observe in everyday life.'"

**HOW TO DO THE ACTIVITY:** Students should be given about five minutes to read the selection and write a brief response to the question. After the allotted time, ask several students to share their responses. It is likely that a number of students (and very likely more boys than girls) will respond in much like the following manner:

"When I get out of the shower my eyeglasses fog up from the condensation."

"When we are driving on a cold and rainy day, the glass inside the car will get all foggy like this."

You may wish to display one or both of these responses on an overhead, instead of having students share their own responses at this point.

On the overhead, chalkboard, or a flip chart, record the question to which students had been asked to respond. Ask someone to underline the part of the question to which the above responses were an answer. Students should quickly see that, in fact, only one component of the response ("a condition that you observe in everyday life") has been addressed.

Have students identify all other parts of the question and key cue words. Students should recognize that a complete response must describe the investigation, make explicit how it functions as a model, and also describe a similar condition under which the same phenomenon is evident. Thus, a complete response might be: "In this investigation, the surface of the colder

## 69. More or Less

**Purpose** To determine the effects of surface temperature on dew formation.

**Materials** clock
glass bottle
jar large enough for the bottle to fit inside
ice
paper towels

**Procedure**

■ Wrap your hands around the bottle and hold it for 2 minutes. You want as much of your skin to touch the glass as possible.

■ Exhale on the outside of the bottle.

■ Observe the surface of the bottle.

■ Fill the jar one-half full with water and add 4 to 5 ice cubes.

■ Set the bottle in the icy water for 2 minutes.

■ Remove the bottle and dry the outside with a paper towel.

■ Exhale on the outside of the bottle.

**Results** The surface of the warm bottle clouds over when the exhaled breath touches it, but the cloud quickly disappears, leaving a dry surface. The cloud formed on the cold bottle by the exhaled breath turns into tiny drops of water. The entire surface of the cold bottle clouds if the humidity of the air is high.

**Why?** Water vapor from your exhaled breath condenses (changes into a liquid) on the surface of both bottles. The

154

warm surface supplies energy for the tiny water droplets to quickly evaporate (change into a vapor). The tiny droplets on the cold surface group together, forming large drops of water. Cold surfaces collect more water drops (dew) than do warmer surfaces. If the surface is too warm, water vapor in the air striking the surface will not condense at all, and if there is a collection of moisture, it quickly evaporates.

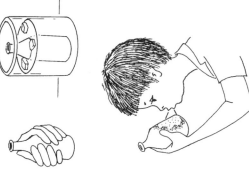

155

*Figure 10.1 An investigation that models a scientific phenonemon.*

From Janice VanCleave, *Earth Science for Every Kids.* ©1991. John Wiley and Sons. Reprinted by permission of John Wiley and Sons.

bottle gets cloudy from the warm, moist breath. This is a model of the process of condensation, which we might see when we leave our glasses, which had been at room temperature, on a counter in the bathroom while we take a warm shower. The glass will get cloudy just like the surface of the bottle did."

Give students the opportunity to examine their own, and a classmate's, response, and check that they have included information that addresses all component cues.

# VARIATIONS/EXTENSIONS: SOME SUGGESTIONS

While the example given was science-oriented, this same behavior may be observed when students respond to complex questions in mathematics and social studies as well. Typically, these question call upon students to demonstrate their understanding of skills and processes and also to apply and extend these understandings. Across the content areas, students need multiple opportunities to "unpack" questions like these that call for the integration of text-based and personal or prior knowledge. Because many real-life situations lend themselves to the integration of knowledge, you might begin by describing a scenario to introduce a "double-barreled" question. For example:

SCENARIO I (MATHEMATICS): Matthew's parents want to take some photographs at his middle school graduation. Because they want a wide array of photos for their family album, they decide to rearrange the family members—Matthew, his little sister, and both parents—in a variety of ways for each shot.

QUESTION: "How could you use your knowledge of a formula we've read about and studied to determine the minimum number of photos that would need to be taken in order to represent Matthew, his mother, father, and little sister, in all possible combinations?"

You are likely to find that in this instance, many students, particularly boys, will simply get to the heart of the matter and solve the problem; however, the critical cue "how" calls for an analysis of process and not simply the resultant product.

SCENARIO II (SOCIAL STUDIES): Following the 2000 presidential election, various constituent groups raised questions about the fairness and accuracy of the voting process.

QUESTION: "Use what you've read and what you know about elections and constitutional rights to explain what processes might be employed to examine the issues in this situation and to resolve them in order to ensure that subsequent elections proceed judiciously."

# Reality Check

Because our students are reading content-specific texts, we may feel confident that they're developing the skills needed to read and make connections between, and extensions from, ideas and information in the core content areas. Many textbooks and other reading resources in science, mathematics, and social studies, however, only pose questions that call for information location and retrieval.

Select at random a set of end-of-chapter or end-of-unit questions that appear in your students' textbooks. Determine if any of these at all require that students make connections between text-based ideas and information and their own ideas, observations, and experiences. Are they asked to reflect upon and reevaluate prior knowledge, and to apply and extend ideas in a real-world context? Supplementing textbook questions with at least some "double-barreled" or "triple-barreled" ones will help ensure that your students don't jump hastily to the perceived "answer," ignoring the process as they do so.

# PART THREE

# BOYS AND GIRLS AS WRITERS: WHAT WE CAN DO

Just as boys and girls demonstrate differing preferences and strengths as readers, so, too, they demonstrate differences as writers. In fact, many of the gendered patterns in children's reading discussed in the preceding parts of the book have direct parallels in boys' and girls' approaches to writing. Some of the most obvious parallels include differences in choices of topics, ways of positioning and developing characters, pace and structure of stories, treatment of conflict and emotion, and the kinds of relationships between writer and reader. For example, boys often choose both to read and to write high-action adventures that feature a single heroic male protagonist, sometimes in the company of a buddy or buddies, whereas girls more often prefer stories that emphasize context and connection, almost never resorting to violence to resolve a conflict. These conspicuous and pervasive differences in writing are, in fact, what first drew our attention to the ways boys and girls can be seen, in Elaine Millard's words, as "differently literate."

Boys' and girls' differing approaches to writing are not confined to expressive writing either. Only a few hours spent browsing through students' classroom reports will likely turn up some of the characteristics that many teachers have come to see as gender markers. Boys' preference for directness and brevity, focus on action, and indifference to elaboration characterizes not only their expressive but also their informative and persuasive writing. And in both fiction and nonfiction, some girls can become so engrossed in the everyday or in exploring the nuances of relationships that they neglect important elements of content that a reader is likely to value.

Coupling observations such as these with our extensive experience in the teaching of writing, we have devised a number of strategies that enable teachers to help both boys and girls become more confident and competent writers. These strategies address such components of writing as development, point of view, establishment of authority, and choice. Just as the strategies described in Part II were based on the belief that all readers can benefit from reflecting on their habits and preferences, developing flexibility, and expanding their repertoires, the activities and suggestions that follow in Part III reflect our conviction that all writers can benefit from becoming more thoughtful and deliberate about the choices they make, developing flexibility, and expanding the number and types of tools available to them.

# 11
# ENHANCING EXPRESSIVE WRITING

One of the most striking differences between the texts created by boys and girls is that boys' narratives tend to take the form of an undeveloped sequence of events. In these pieces, the movement of the storyline is typically signaled by "then...then...then." Skilled writers, by contrast, possess various techniques to make their stories and characters come alive by evoking images, impressions, and recollections of real or imagined events. They use these techniques not only to convey "what happened," but also what characters think and feel and how they interact with each other, creating stories that are richer and more meaningful. Three essential techniques include descriptive detail, dialogue, and reflection (what writer Barry Lane in *After the End* [1993] calls "thoughtshots").

The following activity, "Pass the Bag," helps all students to experience the ways that descriptive detail, dialogue, and reflection can enhance narrative. In this activity, students will take turns selecting color-coded "tickets" that direct them to use different strategies to contribute to a group-generated story.

## PASS THE BAG

**HOW TO GET READY:**

- ◆ Prepare strips of paper in three different colors, totaling about twice the number of students in the group. Place these "tickets" in a large paper bag.

- ◆ On a flip chart or the chalkboard, post a color key indicating which color represents each type of text development—descriptive detail, dialogue, or reflection.

**SUGGESTED GROUPING:** whole class

**HOW TO INTRODUCE THE ACTIVITY (SAY/DO):** "Although writers often work by themselves, sometimes they collaborate to create a story, poem or play. Today, you will be creating a group-generated story, one that I will start and you will continue by adding to the narrative sequence of events. However, in moving the story forward, you will need to use one of three types of development that writers use—descriptive detail, dialogue, or reflection. The color of the ticket you draw from the bag when it's passed to you will tell you which type of development to use."

Illustrate each type of development with examples (see Step 2 below) and engage students in generating some examples in response to a "starter" you offer or to a moment from a familiar story.

**HOW TO DO THE ACTIVITY:**

**Step 1:** Lead off with an opening line or two, to establish key story elements (characters, setting, problem). For example: "Many years ago, in a small village by the sea, a young boy lived with his very old grandparents...."

**Step 2:** Pass the bag to the first student, who must pull a ticket from the bag. The student should consult the key and then add one or more sentences to develop the story accordingly, for example:

- *descriptive detail*: "His grandparents were so old that small birds had made nests in their wrinkles."

- *dialogue*: "Each morning, when he rose, the boy would greet his grandparents by exclaiming loudly, 'Look honored Grandparents, the sun greets you with gold in his arms.' 'Ahhh,' they'd murmur, we are already rich with long life."

- *reflection:* "Often, the young boy would gaze at his grandparents and wonder to himself what he would do if they were not there to care for him."

**Step 3:** After offering the addition to the story prompted by his or her "ticket," the first student should pass the bag to a neighbor, who must draw a new ticket. Based on the color key drawn, this next student will continue the story, using the appropriate type of development to extend or expand upon what has already been said and to move the story forward. Every so often, you may need to take back the bag and add or redirect an event in the story's sequence.

**Subsequent Steps:** The story should continue until either everyone has had a turn, all tickets are used, or the story seems to come to a logical end. If the story ends before everyone has had a turn, you may wish to begin a second story or resume the same activity at another time to give the remaining students an opportunity to participate.

**Additional Steps (Optional):**

1. Tape-record the oral storytelling and transcribe the group story. Give students a copy of the story and invite them to revise by adding to, deleting, moving or changing the ways the story is developed.

2. Students can continue this activity in smaller groups, and then present their completed stories to the rest of the class. Individual students in each small group can continue to take tickets from a smaller bag or act as the "voice" for each type of development (descriptive detail, dialogue, reflection).

# VARIATIONS/EXTENSIONS

## Three Times Better

The same tools that students used to develop a communal story in "Pass the Bag"—descriptive detail, dialogue, and reflection—can also be used by them to revise and improve a story in draft form. After reintroducing and giving a few examples of these types of development, distribute a bare-bones story (see "War Story," page 96) or invite students to select a work in progress. Students can work independently or in pairs to add whichever sorts of development they wish. Invite students to share a portion of the "before" and "after" versions of the story and discuss the impact of the different kinds of development and the effects of focusing on one, another, or all three techniques.

To make these three development techniques a regular part of the writing process in your classroom, give each of your students three markers in the same colors that you have used in "Pass the Bag" to indicate descriptive detail, dialogue, and reflection. When students respond to a peer's draft (or review one of their own for that matter), they can identify missed opportunities for development and use the colored markers to signal the type of development that might enhance the text.

While "then, then, then" stories are more often written by boys, we also noticed this tendency to string together undeveloped events in one distinctly "feminine" story structure we often observed in our research and that has been documented by others as well—the personal narrative that centers around school and home (Adler, 1994; Gilbert, 1994; Kamler, 1993; Peterson, 1998). Girls' calm reportage of everyday events may leave readers feeling as if something is missing. For these sorts of stories, as well, detail, dialogue, and reflection are the remedy we prescribe; they work well both to slow down the often frenetic pace of boys' stories and to quicken the pulse of some of the "small stories" penned by girls.

When using one of these "small stories" as a classroom model, we recommend that you help students first identify a "pulse point"—a particular action or event, even a slight one, upon which the story might turn. If there is none evident, invite students to add one. Then, demonstrate to students how they might use dialogue, descriptive detail, and reflection to quicken the pace and energize the story, highlighting a problem solved, goal reached, or challenge met. (See Figure 11.1 for annotated example.)

## Ways of Saying

Very often, when students introduce dialogue, they do so simply by repeating "he said, she said." The verbs used to introduce dialogue, however, can be important tools for establishing character. Adverbs that modify "ways of saying" further help to convey mood, tone, time, intent, and personality. A mini-lesson on verbs that do the talking, and the adverbs that enhance and give flavor to those verbs, can provide students with the tools for some subtle but powerful development of their expressive writing.

## "WAR STORY"

I'm in the army and we are going to war. We went in to battle.  It was bad. I

have been shooting but I am still going. There are 10 people left in my

platoon. We are low on food and ammo. We are still fighting. We are heading

back to base.  We are about 5 or 10 miles from the base. We are so tired we

rest but two of us have to stand guard. Here they come shooting at us. There

is like 30 or 40 of them and 10 of us so we all shoot. All is a good shot and we

get away but two of my men got shot, one killed one badly injured. We are

almost to the base.  It's about 2 or 3 miles. There it is. We are all 9 of us back

to the base.

From *Reading, Writing, and Gender* by Goldberg and Roswell (© 2002).
Permission to duplicate for classroom use is granted by Eye On Education, Larchmont, NY.

## The Cookie Maker

Once I made a chocolate cookie. I put it in the freezer for a half hour to

make it big and thick. After that I took it out and put some chocolates on it. *Just imagine what she looked like! "That's it," my sister exclaimed. "No more baking for me."*

Then my sister tried it and it exploded all over her face with chocolate. So

she took a bath and then she ate dinner with me. We played tag, and then *All night long my sister dreamed about the chocolate explosion.*

we got ready for bed. Then it was morning and we got up and we ate, got

dressed and went to school. After school was over, we went home and did *The mud puddles there made my sister think about chocolate. "Come on," she suddenly cried. "Let's go home and try again."*

our homework, then went to the park to play. Then we made more chocolate

*We were lucky and the cookies wound up*
cookies. *in our mouths and not on our faces.*

---

Through discussion, one class decided that the "pulse point" in this story was
the exploding cookie, which in the original version of the story is mentioned in
passing and then abandoned for an undeveloped list of events (then, then,
then...). With dialogue, more descriptive detail, and some "thoughtshots,"
students enlivened this story and emphasized its inherent challenge and
message--if at first you don't succeed (even at something as ordinary as
cookie-baking), try again.

*Figure 11.1 An enhanced "small story."*

# The "Four M's"

Extending upon his metaphor of writing as driving, Peter Thomas (1997) suggests that when writing, boys can profit from occasional road signs to "Stop, Slow Down, and Look Around." Thomas names these narrative controls the Four M's—Motive, Manner, Mood and Morality. He thus gives alternative language to, and a way to approach, the teaching of development in expressive writing. We like the idea of using his "Four M's" when discussing draft-stage stories, plays and poems, especially with middle school students. You might invite students to find opportunities in their texts to elaborate upon motive (details to answer why a character acts a certain way), manner and mood (details that evoke more precisely how actions unfold and are perceived by the character and others) and morality (details that convey the impact and consequences of actions and events). Demonstrate through modeling, collaborative writing, and sharing, that texts can be improved by linking actions with thought, feeling and motivation, and by connecting events to the setting in which they occur, the consequences of the action, and the reactions of other characters. Boys in particular can be prompted to vary their focus to include the effects of rampant heroics on others—or to complicate their view of heroism. More advanced writers, boys and girls alike, can be supported in their efforts to do this with subtlety and suggestion, hinting at tastes or character (for example, by describing an item in a character's wardrobe, or a style of walking) or by alluding to a conversation, rather than by explicit statement.

Start by brainstorming "ways of saying." Then come up with a way to modify each one and record these for display on a flipchart or the chalkboard. Some examples are:

| | | | |
|---|---|---|---|
| cry | *pitifully* | whimper | *softly* |
| shout | *exuberantly* | murmur | *seductively* |
| exclaim | *joyfully* | giggle | *shyly* |
| bellow | *angrily* | moan | *painfully* |
| sigh | *wistfully* | gasp | *suddenly* |

Next, have students write a narrative in which they use dialogue to move events through time. Encourage them to draw upon the posted options or other "ways of saying." This approach works particularly well for a piece of historical fiction based in a period of time the class has studied (see Figure 11.2). Because students will have various facts and details at their disposal and will not have to put as much energy into inventing events, they can concentrate on evoking interchange through dialogue.

### The Harsh Winter at Valley Forge

On a brisk evening, Hank awoke from his freezing cold hut to find mounds of snow lying on the ground outside. He shivered and grabbed a brown blanket hoping that it would keep him warm. Hank thought that if more snow came down, it would mean trouble for the Americans that stayed at Valley Forge. He decided that he would go see how his pal Tobias was holding up. Tobias lived three huts down from where Hank and 12 other people slept.

Cautiously, Hank arose from his damp straw bed, and stepped over several men who were still asleep. He creep silently outside the hut. He saw a city of huts scattered about the land. Nonchalantly, Hank headed towards Tobias's hut. The wind blew harshly in his face, but this didn't stop him. Suddenly, Hank stopped walking. There was Tobias. He was a young tall man with light brown hair. He came from his home in  to join the Continental Army. He was very courageous. Tobias was talking with Tom. Tom was a frail young man who came from South Carolina to fight in the war. Tom had once been a planter, but he thought freedom was more important. Hank dashed behind a large hut to hear the conversation. He could not believe his ears.

"I am leaving Valley Forge tomorrow!" Tobias announced.

"You can't leave Valley Forge  General Washington and the rest of the army need you!" Tom exclaimed.

"I know," Tobias responded, " but I can't stand this place. I think that if there is no water to drink and hardly any food to eat, then we will eventually perish. I am not going to give my life up for an army that just sits here and waits to die."

Tom responded, "I understand what you are saying, but hundreds have died here already. This makes the army decrease in size. If you go, then this will be one less man gone that we can't afford to lose."

Tobias replied, "I don't care. Besides my life, I have a family back at home that needs me. They think that I have perished by now. I want to go home and tell them that I am alive and well."

"But what about your friends?" Tom questioned strongly, "Do you want to leave them behind? Do you want to leave them here to die?"

"Tom" Tobias asked stiffly, "Would you like to stay here in the bitter cold weather with no food or water? Would you like to stay here where the smoke fills the air? Do you like how the roofs of our only shelter, straw huts, leak with rain? Do you like how Smallpox and Typhoid Fever sweep through each straw hut they reach? You like it here, don't you?"

"No, but I just don't care anymore," Tom replied.

"Look Tom," Tobias interjected, "This has been one harsh winter. If I stay here I might get the least of my worries, frostbite."

Hank heard them bickering over staying or leaving. He decided he'd ought to jump in. Hank jumped out of his hiding place and said, "Tobias, I couldn't help to overhear your little argument. I just want to ask you one question. Do you care about your freedom? Do you want to stay under the King's power forever? That's what we are here for. We are fighting for that freedom that we yearn for."

Tobias smiled and said, "He is right! I love the thought of freedom. I'll stay!"

Tom gave Hank a pat on the back.

"Thanks, Hank! You saved a soldier," he said.

With that, Hank returned to his hut and covered himself with a blanket. He fell into a deep sleep.

*Figure 11.2 A student makes history come to life through descriptive detail, reflection, and dialogue introduced with varied "ways of saying."*

Some teachers have found it useful to make a display of "ways of saying" a permanent classroom resource in the form of a poster or word wall. In one classroom we visited, students working in the writing corner could reach into an envelope stuffed with laminated cards with options for "what to say instead of said" (see Figure 11.3) to help them enhance language choices when writing expressive texts.

*Figure 11.3 What to say instead of "said."*

## Seeing Double or Even Triple: Double/Triple Entry Journals

We know from our own lives that we don't always say or do all the things that reflect what we're thinking. Students can capitalize on that awareness by creating two- or three-dimensional stories that incorporate action, dialogue, and reflection. First, model the process by displaying on an overhead transparency or chart paper a brief description of a situation that would be familiar to students, such as the following:

> The kitchen door slammed as I ran inside and went straight to the refrigerator. As I grabbed the bottle of milk I yelled, "Hi Mom, I'm home." I gulped down some milk and went for the cookies.
>
> "Hi dear," my Mom replied. "I'm so glad your home. I have such a nice surprise for you."

"Uh-huh," I answered, with my mouth full of crumbs. "Man, I'm hungry," I thought.

"Your Aunt Hilda is here for a visit!" Mom exclaimed.

"Oh great," I replied, shoving another cookie in my mouth. I was really annoyed. "Guess I won't get to try out the new computer game that Carlos lent me," I thought to myself. "Be right in, Mom," I offered.

Create a three column chart and use it to list actions, dialogue, and reflections that your students identify in the description. Point out that stories often move forward and are developed in these various ways. To help them explore ways of weaving together action, dialogue, and reflection, students will next draft their own stories in columnar form.

It may be easiest to start with only two columns, using a double-entry format to draft portions of text using two of the three types of development. Students should fold a journal page (or separate piece of paper) in half, lengthwise. On one side, they will record all the actions in their story (what happened). On the other, they will interject, at appropriate points, what was said (dialogue) or what was going on inside the characters' minds (reflection). On another occasion, students should do the same exercise, but change the second column to the form of development (dialogue or reflection) that they had not already employed. Be sure to build in time for sharing and discussion, so that students receive confirmation of the impact of developing events and actions, as well as suggestions for additional revision/refinement.

Once students have had the opportunity to try out both types of development, switch to a tri-fold format, so that students can fully flesh out the stories they write with what happened, what was said, and what was thought or imagined.

## Pause and Post-It

During a unit on insects, third-grade students were asked by their classroom teacher to write a story about what would happen if their science teacher turned them into bugs. Kristin and Carla, elementary school resource teachers, found that almost all of the students, but the boys in particular, marched through their version of "a bug's life" in "then…then…then" fashion, recording an undeveloped sequence of events. Recognizing that the radical shift in perspective to an insect's point of view made dialogue unlikely (unless it was a plaintive, "hey you, up there" called from the sidewalk to a full-sized classmate), they decided to use the stories as an occasion for a mini-lesson on reflection.

They began by generating ways of thinking out loud—the internal equivalent of "ways of saying." Kristen started the students off with "I thought." Within minutes, students had brainstormed over a dozen other ways of signaling "internal dialogue" and reflection:

| | |
|---|---|
| I thought, "_____." | I hoped |
| I wondered, "_____." | I expected |
| I asked myself, "_____." | I guessed |

| | |
|---|---|
| I said to myself, "_____." | I puzzled over |
| I exclaimed inside, "_____." | I imagined |
| I wondered whether (if, when) | I pondered |
| I questioned whether (if) | I feared |

Kristen and Carla then modeled the use of a set of small Post-it notes with one of these leads written on each. Working in pairs, students shared their rough drafts and helped each other to discover places where the protagonist, in his or her insect state, had occasion to reflect upon something or talk to him or herself. Using the Post-it notes, students marked their own and their peers' drafts at points that could be enhanced through this sort of development (see Figure 11.4). Not only did the activity generate lots of laughter and energy, but it led to more richly developed and engaging stories.

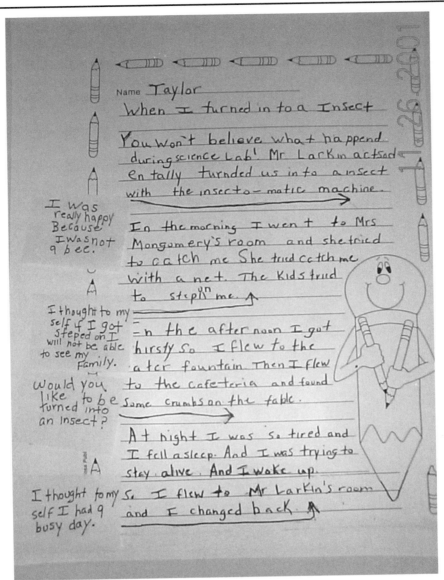

When I turned into an Insect (revised version)

You won't believe what happened during Science Lab. Mr. Larkin accidentally turned me into an insect with the insecto-matic machine. I was really happy because I was a butterfly and not a bee. In the morning I went to Mrs. Montgomery's room and she tried to catch me with a net. The kids tried to step on me. I thought to myself, "If I get stepped on I will not be able to see my family." In the afternoon, I got thirsty. So I flew to the water fountain. Then I flew to the cafeteria where I found some crumbs on the table. Would you like to be turned into an insect and have to eat crumbs? At night, I was so tired and I fell asleep. I was just trying to stay alive. Then I woke up and I flew back to Mr. Larkin's room and changed back into a boy. I thought to myself, "I had a busy day."

*Figure 11.4 A student uses Post-Its with reflection leads to enhance his rough draft about "A Bug's Life."*

# 12

# GETTING TO THE POINT VERSUS GUIDING READERS TOWARD THE POINT WHEN WRITING TO INFORM

The lack of development evident in the bare-bones stories of many boys is characteristic not only of their expressive writing but also of writing they do for other purposes—writing to inform or persuade. In fact when Misty, a middle school teacher, showed her male students data on the relative achievement of girls and boys as writers and asked for their reaction, they responded that "writing is more of a girl thing." Regardless of their purpose for writing, boys explained that they liked to "get to the point." One boy summed up the group's sentiments by declaring, "Don't expect 'long' written work."

While writing should not be measured with a ruler in any classroom or assessment context, it is safe to say that many boys, and certainly some girls, miss opportunities to extend, expand, and elaborate upon their ideas when writing to inform. Often, students' informative texts read like a list of facts or details, a pouring out of what they know about a particular topic. Beginning with "Stretch It," the following activities provide students with some tools and techniques such as internalizing readers' questions, using anecdotes and specific examples, and incorporating quotations, that enhance the development of informative writing.

## STRETCH IT

HOW TO GET READY: Compose a brief paragraph to explain or describe something you know well (your family, a hobby, a recent trip) but about which your students are likely to know little, and make a transparency of it. Make sure the paragraph is "bare-bones," leaving many unanswered questions. When Gail does this activity, for example, she often shares a paragraph about her children like this one:

I have two sons, and Justin is the younger of the two. He is a college student. He really likes to read and write. Justin is very different from me in some ways but like me in many ways, too. While Ethan, my older son, has turned out almost exactly the way I imagined he would, Justin always has been, and continues to be, full of surprises.

SUGGESTED GROUPING: whole class

HOW TO INTRODUCE THE ACTIVITY (SAY/DO): "Since I thought you might like to know more about my family, I wrote this paragraph" (read from your transparency the text of your bare-bones paragraph). "Okay, so now you know everything you want or need to know about my family (hobby, trip, etc.), right?" (Elicit reactions). "I've probably raised more questions than I've answered. To satisfy your curiosity, I have to put some "meat" on the "bones" of my text."

HOW TO DO THE ACTIVITY: Distribute or display the "Stretch It" cues (see page 107). Ask students to reread your paragraph and identify all the places where they might want to inject some of these questions in order to learn more. As they call upon you to "stretch" your text by asking these questions, respond with appropriate details, examples, and anecdotes—resources that develop informative writing. Then ask students, "What effect do the additions I've made have?" Guide students to see that addition of details, examples, and anecdotes makes ideas more interesting, more complete, more important or more powerful. Through discussion, make sure that students understand how to figure out the points in their texts that lend themselves to stretching (the places where they can anticipate that readers might have questions and want to know more).

The next step is to have students use the "stretch-it" cues to guide revision of their own draft-stage writing. First review the "stretch-it" cues, and then have students pair up and use the cues as a peer-response resource, identifying for their partners the places within their texts that raise questions, and noting the questions in particular that come to mind.

## VARIATIONS/EXTENSIONS

Students are likely to be most comfortable, initially, using specific details to extend and expand their ideas when writing to inform. If students are using only one or two techniques to "stretch it," direct their attention towards examples and anecdotes as well.

## Examining Examples

Gather from student samples an array of general statements and share these on a chalkboard, overhead, flip chart, or handout. Elicit a variety of examples that extend and expand upon each idea and that demonstrate that general words and phrases can be interpreted and exemplified in many ways. The following passages illustrate the ways that examples can be used to develop descriptions of individuals:

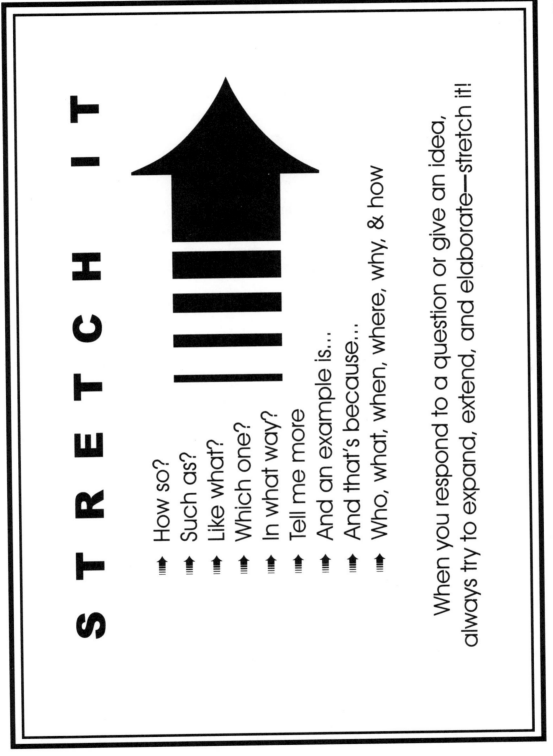

# STRETCH IT

↑ How so?

↑ Such as?

↑ Like what?

↑ Which one?

↑ In what way?

↑ Tell me more

↑ And an example is...

↑ And that's because...

↑ Who, what, when, where, why, & how

When you respond to a question or give an idea, always try to expand, extend, and elaborate—stretch it!

- Even though my Grandma lives far away, her grandchildren are never far from her mind. Whenever she is out shopping, she's likely to say, "Oh, Chris would like that," or "Tiffany could really use one of those."

- That coach is really interested in her players. I've seen her call for a "time-out" and pull aside one of the members of the team for a quiet chat when she knows that player has been having a difficult day.

- Marco sometimes gets in over his head….Even when he should say "no thanks, my plate's full," he'll take on another project or work with another committee or school publication, just because they need some help.

## Any Anecdotes?

Sometimes, instead of elaborating upon an idea with specific details, we choose to tell a story that illustrates or exemplifies that idea in a particularly apt way. It is for good reason that many of us associate anecdotes with older people, people whose story-telling reflects a lifetime of experience and observation. Why not make older adults partners then, in students' writing?

Begin by telling your class, "I'm going to tell you a little story…" and then recount a personal experience. Here's one we've shared, for example, that illustrates the adage "Love makes fools of us all":

> Years ago, when I was in fifth grade, I had a crush on a boy named Peter. He was the cutest boy in my class, and he was smart too. I really, really wanted him to notice me. At the end of the year, during the fifth grade party, Peter asked me to dance. I was thrilled. As Peter guided me around the dance floor, he leaned close to me and said, "You know, there's something I just realized." My heart fluttered. "What?" I asked. "You can tell me." Peter hesitated and then said, "I don't know. It's something I never knew before." Breathlessly, I urged Peter, "You can tell me." "Well," Peter finally responded, "I just realized that you have hair on your arms."

Tell students that brief accounts of an incident like this one or the like the one you choose to tell are called *anecdotes,* and ask students to identify the "big ideas" illustrated by the anecdote you have recounted. Then introduce the strategy of using and anecdote to illustrate a generalization.

Share with students a number of generalizations or "words of wisdom" that have traditionally been used to guide thinking and behavior. Some examples might be:

- With luck and hard work you can accomplish almost anything

- Sometimes people are stronger on the inside than they seem on the outside

- Sometimes people who seem funny are really very sad

- If at first you don't succeed, try and try again

- It's never too late

Have students identify several generalizations that they find most powerful and brainstorm related ideas and associations. The brainstorm list should be copied and given to students as "raw material" to use later. Meanwhile, have each student pick one generalization they'd like to explore further as a writer. Students should then interview three or four older adults to ask if they have a little story to tell that would support that idea. While listening, or immediately afterwards, they should jot down some notes.

Then, using their own ideas, the ideas generated by the class, and one or more anecdotes, they should write to inform other students about their "words of wisdom." These essays can be collected in a big book called "Writing to Live By." Students have written to inform, and have used the experiences and observations of their elders to help teach a lesson.

## All Together Now

Find or create a brief informative piece that needs more development, like this sample:

> The cafeteria is a really uncomfortable place to be. We could do some things to make it a better place. Then students would like to be there more. We could use it for lots of different things.

Discuss and model: "Where might we add some vivid descriptive detail? Where might we add some specific examples? Where might we add an anecdote?"

As a next step, have students identify a community problem that has been featured recently in a local paper. Encourage them to identify places in the text where it would be helpful to have some additional descriptive details or examples.

## Look Who's Talking

Students can borrow a common newspaper strategy to help informative pieces come alive—by using direct quotes from credible and appropriate people. Eyewitnesses, people with firsthand experience, experts, or "people-in-the-street" are all good sources of quotations that extend and expand ideas and information. Look at informative pieces from newspapers and magazines to see this in practice. Identify embedded quotes and discuss how they work to enhance the writing.

As part of this mini-lesson, make sure students understand it's not just what is said, but who is doing the talking that's important. So, for example, you can tell students, "Don't just say, 'I talked to someone who said the kids at that school are poorly behaved' when you can tell me 'Mrs. Sherman, the guidance counselor at the local middle school, said the students there are poorly behaved.'"

Brainstorm with students to arrive at the kinds of authorities they are likely to quote and different ways to establish the reason for a reader to listen to and believe these speakers. For example:

- Jasper Jones, author of *Great Poets of the Twentieth Century*... (author of a book)

- Sonya Sanchez, director of the Save the Wilderness Foundation... (leader of a group)

- Edward Gaines, a neighbor who often saw Nikki after school... (eyewitness)

As a reading/writing connection, you may wish to ask students to identify quotations in a newspaper or magazine article and engage in debate over the credibility or bias of those who are quoted.

# 13

# ASSERTION AND NEGOTIATION: HELPING STUDENTS "MAKE A CASE" WHEN WRITING TO PERSUADE

We believe strongly that there exists an affinity between action research and explorations into issues involving literacy and gender. Perhaps because classroom teachers are closest to the everyday ways that the students they teach are "doing gender," or perhaps because currently espoused theories are deemed inadequate by many teachers, even in the absence of a directive to do so, teacher-researchers frequently make gender a focus of their research. Not surprisingly, the illustrative account in a recent article on action research of one teacher's "'aha' moment," when she realized that research questions were all around her, involved language and gender. According to Power & Hubbard (1999), when Kelli Clark asked her students to assume the role of emperor towards the end of the demise of ancient Rome, and to write a decree that issued orders that would save the empire, she little expected what occurred. Although the class had discussed and role-played the use of authoritative language, Kelli recalled that when she read her students' drafts, she discovered that:

> Several students engaged in lengthy, grandiose descriptions of their personal authority and what might happen to their subjects if they did not comply with the decree. I read as the self-described "Supreme and Undaunted Ruler of the Universe," "Leader of the Assassins," and "John the Decapitator" blew up, savagely beat, and otherwise abused the unfortunate imaginary plebeians and patricians. As I began to wonder if I'd over-emphasized the authority issue, I started seeing papers that passively requested something be done. The Most Superior Being on Earth "suggested" that the people "do" something. The Ruler Most High said, "I think you should...." (35)

Kelli's assignment had triggered a very common disparity between the persuasive strategies of boys and girls. As she noted, "Here was aggression and inappropriate levels of violence from my sixth- and seventh-grade boys. Here was Ophelia pleading for the salvation of

Rome, even as she had been given complete authority and power to toss the populace a life-line. Overall, 35% of the boys and 30% of the girls showed these gender patters in their writing. Not one boy wrote in the passive voice. Not one girl blew up a plebeian" (35-36).

The following activity, "Who's in Charge" was developed with Kelli's students in mind. This activity, as well as others in this chapter, may help students to examine more closely the language that they use when they're expected to take charge—to use persuasive language and development strategies to compel their audience to think or act a certain way.

# WHO'S IN CHARGE?

HOW TO GET READY: Determine a suitable scenario based on a work of literature or a historical period familiar to your students. Some possible scenarios include the following:

- for intermediate students: "Imagine you've been appointed principal for a day. Think about the way things work in school and about changes you might like to see happen at school. Use one of the ways of expressing 'who's in charge' to fill in the sign to tell others (students and teachers) how things should be at school."

- for intermediate students: "Imagine you are an explorer in charge of an expedition to discover new lands. Think about the way you believe things should work during the expedition and about changes you would like to see in how things are being done. Use one of the ways of expressing 'who's in charge' to fill in the sign to tell others (workers and serving staff, soldiers, etc.) how things should be during the expedition."

- for middle school students in English language arts, in response to Sachar's *Holes*: "Imagine you are the Warden at the detention center, Camp Green Lake. You are not satisfied with how hole digging is progressing. Use one of the ways of expressing 'who's in charge' to complete the sign by telling the boys at the detention center what you expect of them."

- for middle school students in social studies: "Imagine you are the leader of a wagon train, headed across the Oregon Trail. Think about the way you believe things should work while you are all heading west and about changes you might like to see in how things are being done. Use one of the ways of expressing 'who's in charge' to fill in the sign to tell others (men, women, children, soldiers, etc.) how things should be while you are all heading west."

SUGGESTED GROUPING: individual, small group, whole group.

HOW TO INTRODUCE THE ACTIVITY (SAY/DO): "Over the past few [weeks, months], we have witnessed individuals, both real and fictional, attempt to control or shape the behavior of others around them. Today, I'd like you to imagine you are someone from [history, literature] who imagines himself/herself to be, or who actually is, 'in charge.'"

Introduce the scenario of your choice. Then, distribute copies of the "I'm In Charge" form (see page 114) and give students sufficient time to read it over. You may wish to call on one or more students to read the options aloud.

"Select one of the ways of expressing 'who's in charge' that you think is appropriate in this situation. Then, fill in the sign to tell others how you think things should be done. Be sure to identify the approach you've chosen with a check mark."

**HOW TO DO THE ACTIVITY:** After students have selected a form of expressing "who's in charge" and completed their sign, give them the opportunity to share their work with group members. Give teams five to ten minutes to develop a list of words and phrases that they feel helped to make the sign compelling. These lists should become the basis for class discussion on persuasive language and effective ways to express assertions, demands, and expectations. This activity also encourages discussion about appropriate and inappropriate forms for expressing ideas about the limits of people's behavior.

# VARIATIONS/EXTENSIONS

## Some Mini-Lessons

1.  Conduct a mini-lesson on forms that historical documents that express assertions have taken (e.g., decrees, declarations, proclamations). Have students read two or more examples of such documents, aligned to grade-level curriculum, and discuss:

    - What is the central issue that this document addresses?

    - What position did the author(s) take towards that issue?

    - How did the author(s) want the reader(s) of this document to think, feel, or act?

    - How did the author(s) convey that? What sorts of language did the author(s) use?

    - What sorts of development did the author(s) use to extend/expand ideas?

2.  The above explorations of "Who's in Charge?" lend themselves to extension by discussing and modeling the use of development strategies appropriate to persuasive writing. Students should become aware that to support a position, writers make use of facts, first-hand observations and experiences or perspectives, and warranted generalizations. They try to steer clear of broad generalizations, hearsay, and/or propaganda.

    You may wish to demonstrate types of development for persuasive writing by having the class craft a group piece. Start with a topic that relates to students' own experiences (e.g., your parents don't want you to play video games on school nights). Have them take the position that they disagree with their parents and are trying to convince their parents to change their minds.

    First brainstorm to get reasons; have students pick out the "strong" support. This is a good time to teach the difference between reasons that are specific and credible and those that are too general and don't really say anything or are of questionable credibility.

## I'm In Charge!

☐ <u>Declaration</u>: an announcement; a formal statement or document, sometimes legally binding

☐ <u>Edict</u>: an official decree; a formal command or prohibition; a public notice issued by official authority; a proclamation of a command, law, or rule of conduct by sovereign power or competent authority

☐ <u>Law</u>: the binding custom or practice of a community; rules of conduct enforced by a controlling authority

☐ <u>Manifesto</u>: a public and formal declaration or expression of principles or intentions, usually by a sovereign or person claiming large powers, showing intentions and motives; a statement of policy or opinion issued by an organization, party, or group

☐ <u>Proclamation</u>: a public, authoritative announcement

☐ <u>Proposal</u>: an offer, scheme, plan or bid; a proposition

☐ <u>Rule</u>: a prescribed guide for conduct, action, or usage; uniform or established course or practice

Distinguish strong, logical reasons and evidence (facts, firsthand observations, warranted generalizations) from weak reasons (broad generalizations, unsubstantiated claims, hearsay, propaganda).

After choosing strong support, cluster the reasons into related categories. Use the categories as topic sentences and draft a well-supported group piece.

3. A simple mini-lesson, but one that dramatizes stereotypes about language and gender, involves doing the following:

Record on the chalkboard two different messages, and tell students that you found these posted at two different restaurants you recently patronized.

- No cell phones and/or beepers allowed inside
- Our guests will enjoy their dinners more if you will kindly turn off your cell phone or beeper before entering the dining area. Bon Appetit!

OR

- No smoking allowed
- Fine food tastes better without the seasoning of secondhand smoke

You will generate some lively discussion by asking 1) Which of these (in each pair) do you think was written by a man and which by a woman? Why? and 2) Which of these messages would you be more likely to respond to? Why?

## Good/Better Than/Best

Present a scenario that requires persuading someone to agree with a particular choice. Then, brainstorm in tri-column form to determine what makes that choice "good," "better than," and "the best" out of a variety of choices. Compare the persuasive character of ideas in each column. Students should recognize that just identifying what makes something "good" is not enough to be really compelling. Comparison is needed. (Gail likes to model this with a choice of a favorite dessert to serve at a special event: students might respond well to options for a party theme.)

You may wish instead to order this activity somewhat differently, by having students make a choice and then list things they might say to make their reader/listener agree with their choice. Then, look at the lists and sort the reasons given according to whether each idea showed that the choice was good, better than another choice, or the best of several choices. Again, lead back to the idea that to be persuasive, we must not only convey what makes something good, but also acknowledge competing options and explain why it is the better or best choice out of several we might make.

## Shoe on the Other Foot

Even very young writers can extend their persuasive communications—written or oral—by identifying one objection their audience might have and responding to that objection with some evidence, example, or principle. Practice this orally or by adding to a standard persuasive graphic organizer a section labeled "You may think _____ but I believe_____ because

_____." Be sure to emphasize to your students that what they add in the second part should not simply be a restatement of their position, but rather, some idea or information that responds to the particular issue they have identified as an objection.

## Refutation Wall

Another way to develop persuasive writing is to more comprehensively identify and respond to your audience's most likely objections—that is, to add refutation. A good way to introduce refutation to students is through use of a refutation wall. Start by selecting an engaging issue/problem (e.g., extending a student's bedtime for younger students or, for older ones, changing regulations for new drivers). After identifying various reasons a student might have for seeking a later bedtime, have students brainstorm to come up with some reasons why their parents (the audience for this piece of writing) might not want them to have a later bedtime. Have them write each of these objections on a Post-it note. Then, stick three of the audience's most likely objections on three cardboard boxes (I like to use tissue-box sized or larger) and pile the blocks up; then, come up with a way to refute each objection, and as you do, knock down one block. Soon, what stands between you and what you want is gone! For example:

- objection: You will be too tired for school the next day.
  refutation: I already wake before my alarm goes off, which shows I'm getting all the sleep my body needs.

- objection: You will be crabby.
  refutation: I will head in to bed as soon as I feel myself getting grouchy.

- objection: I need my quiet time.
  refutation: Even though I'll be up later, I'll be sure to stay in my own room, so I won't bother you at all.

# 14

# GET THE PICTURE: DEVELOPMENT AT THE PLANNING STAGE OF WRITING

Although planning and drafting precedes revision when we teach—and our students engage in—"the writing process," attention to development in writing may be most effective when we start backwards, by recognizing what's still missing when students think their texts are "done." The strategies for developing the expressive, informative, and persuasive writing that we have described thus far typically emanate from students' draft-stage work or work that they believe to be in final form.

Through a variety of activities, such as those set out in earlier chapters, students should have come to recognize that development in writing can take many different forms: dialogue, reflection, and descriptive detail in expressive writing; specific details, examples or anecdotes, and quotations in informative writing; and facts, firsthand observations and experiences, and warranted generalizations in persuasive writing. Once students are conversant in these and other ways to extend and expand ideas across purposes for writing, you can help them to consider ways to be more deliberate about development at earlier stages in their writing process—specifically, as part of their planning and prewriting. The coupling of graphic organizers with icons representing ways of extending, expanding, and elaborating in "I-Con Do More" and related activities helps students to discover, early on in their writing process, that they can do more in the way of development.

## I-CON DO MORE

HOW TO GET READY: Based on the particular writing task in which students will be engaged, identify an appropriate graphic organizer that students can use to plan their writing. For example, for a process explanation or narrative, you might pick a sequence chain (see page 118), or for an argument, you might pick a pro/con chart. Prepare copies of the organizer for the whole class and one or two transparency copies.

Use the template of screen bean icons (see page 119) to prepare a transparency; cut apart individual icons that can be used as overlays.

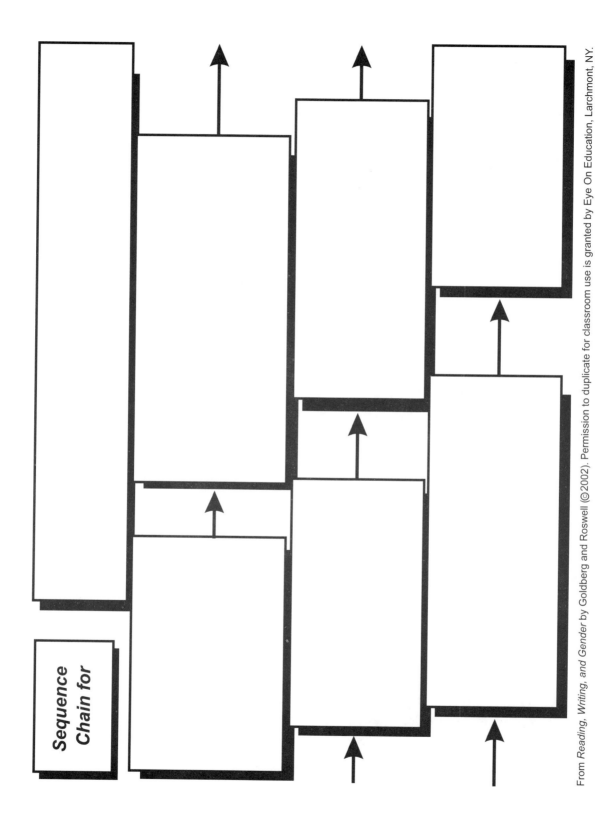

Sequence Chain for

# SCREEN BEAN ICONS

Pose a question

Present an alternative

Issue a warning (caution)

Relay an aside
(between you and me)

Make a suggestion

Share a reflection
("thought-shot")

Provide data

Add a quotation

Convey an image
(picture it)

Step Up
(make a generalization)

Make a projection
(look ahead)

Step Down
(give specific details or examples)

From *Reading, Writing, and Gender* by Goldberg and Roswell (© 2002).
Permission to duplicate for classroom use is granted by Eye On Education, Larchmont, NY.

SUGGESTED GROUPING: individual planning; whole class modeling and discussion

HOW TO INTRODUCE THE ACTIVITY: Set the stage for a piece of informative writing, and then give students the opportunity to use a suitable graphic organizer to plan it. For example, you might have students write to inform younger children how to do or make something that they will find useful in their everyday lives. In this case, some version of a sequence chain would be useful for planning. As students are working, ask one or two students to record their plans on a transparency of the organizer or, if you prefer anonymous models, have on hand a completed transparency.

HOW TO DO THE ACTIVITY: After students have used their organizers to plan their writing (in this case, a process explanation), use an overhead projector to display an example of a completed graphic organizer in which information/ideas are limited to those cued for by the form itself. Typically, students will complete a sequence chain organizer by recording one step of the process they've chosen to write about in each box.

Using only three or four of the transparency icons, introduce students to a few ways to extend and expand their ideas. In this instance, you might display the icons for a warning, an alternative, and an aside. We modeled this activity by developing the steps for making a peanut butter and jelly sandwich (see page 121).

Students will quickly be able to see that these ways of developing their text will lead to richer drafts. Once they have a completed a draft, they may wish to repeat this process, considering places to insert either these forms of development or one or two others as well, such as conveying an image or making a projection.

This activity can be repeated often, varying the use of different development icons each time. In the process, students should be encouraged to compare their written work with peers' and to discuss which types of development seem most appropriate for different purposes for, and forms of, writing. As a consequence, students should recognize that although there is certainly no one right way to extend and expand their ideas, some ways are better suited than others to their intentions as writers and the needs of their readers.

# VARIATIONS/EXTENSIONS: SOME SUGGESTIONS

♦ The use of icons to consider where to develop draft-stage texts, and how to do so, can be applied effectively to expressive writing as well as to informative writing. Of the dozen graphics we've watched teachers use with great success, the ones most applicable to expressive writing are those signaling students to relay an aside, share a reflection, add a quotation, convey an image, and pose a question.

♦ For persuasive writing, we might model use of the icons to signal students to provide data, pose a question, or add a quotation.

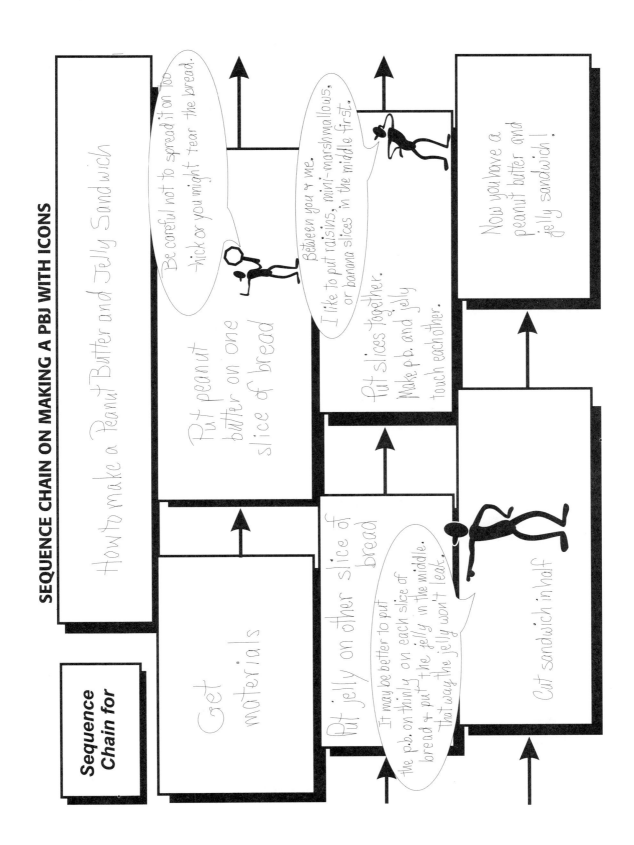

◆ Another variation of this strategy is particularly useful for informative and persuasive writing. All too often, our students string together ideas and reasons that take the form of unelaborated statements. They are sometimes overly general ("boys like rough sports") or overly specific ("boys like rugby and they like football and wrestling too"). To help students understand the need for both general ideas and elaboration, select a completed graphic organizer that has elicited merely a list of ideas or reasons and display it as a transparency. Then, overlay the screen bean icons indicating the need to "step up" (make a generalization) or "step down" (give one or two specific details or examples) where appropriate. Have students suggest ways to make the displayed plan more complete by including both main and subsidiary ideas and examples. One side benefit to this lesson is clarification for students of the difference between general ideas or reasons and the ways we extend, expand, and/or elaborate upon them.

## Icon Conversation

These twelve screen bean icons have become so familiar in a number of schools where we work that they've taken on a life of their own. At Banneker Elementary School, in St. Mary's County, Maryland, children participated in a contest to name the screen bean, who is now referred to across grades as "Extendo." You may meet Extendo at school assemblies (courtesy of one teacher's excellent sewing skills and two dramatically-inclined colleagues in the costumes she created), energetically pantomiming "make a suggestion," "between you and me," or "pose a question," as students take turns sharing their writing with other students and faculty (see Figure 14.1). At Gale-Bailey Elementary School, in Charles County, Maryland, students tape screen beans to authentic texts, such as product packaging, wherever they find evidence of particular ways of extending and expanding ideas, and also use the icons to guide peer response and revision. In several other schools in Charles County, teachers include in their writing prompts the reminder to "be sure to include at least two 'beans'" (a.k.a. ways of developing their writing).

Figure 14.1 *The screen bean icons become a familiar part of writing instruction, to make the process of extending and developing ideas come alive.*

# 15

# A MATTER OF CHOICE/ CHOICE MATTERS TO WRITERS

By the intermediate grades, and certainly in middle school, so much school-based writing is expected to be "academic" in nature that teachers may have little opportunity to learn about students' individual writing preferences. Even when students are given the opportunity to write personal narratives, fiction, or poetry, curriculum mandates often lead teachers to create assignments that are substantially prescribed in terms of topic, purpose for writing, form and information sources (e.g. "use information from the article, 'Storms,' and what you know to write a poem about the weather" or "write about a time when you faced a challenge"). Despite a quarter century of experience with process-oriented writing instruction, a majority of students' writing is still intended for one audience only—the teacher who will evaluate the writing and assign a grade. Small wonder, then, that many boys and girls come to dread writing, and their work, voiceless and formulaic, reflects their lack of engagement.

You may be among the many teachers who, like Lucy Calkins (1994) and Nancie Atwell (1998), are committed to process-oriented and workshop-based writing instruction and who recognize the importance of giving students the opportunity to choose what to write about, in what form, and for whom. Yet, as Barbara Kamler has pointed out, persistent gender stereotypes, combined with students' often limited reading repertoires, can lead to workshop environments that are less "liberating" than we might wish (1993). Kamler cautions that by offering students free choice, we may unwittingly reinforce the most extreme gender differences—boys will more often generate violent, action sequences whereas girls will increasingly limit their topics to home, school, and family. Both our own research and the research of many others shows that boys and girls both tend to choose from fairly limited and often gender-specific topics and only rarely to explore the full array of genres available to them as writers. At the same time, some of the most successful writing, especially by boys, occurs when students step outside of the more familiar genres and experiment with fictionalized news stories, parodies, raps and other forms that draw on visually mediated texts like cartoons, comics, video games, and film.

The following activity, "Charting Choices as Writers," parallels "Charting Choices as Readers" (see Chapter 3), and is designed to enable students to consider the many options available to them and to identify their sometimes limited and gender-bound choices as writers. By first highlighting and then challenging students' habitual approaches to writing, "Charting Choices" gives students opportunities and impetus to build on their strengths in order to take some risks, venture into new territory, and expand their writing repertoires.

## CHARTING CHOICES AS WRITERS

**HOW TO GET READY:** Brainstorm with students to come up with the sorts of choices they might make about topic, audience, purpose, form, and style/tone when writing. You might ask, for example: "What sorts of things do you usually like to write about?" "Who do you usually have in mind as a reader?" "Is there a particular tone you like to take, and what others might you be interested in trying out?" Use this information to create a matrix or "menu" of writing choices, as shown on the next page, and provide each student with a copy. Be sure to allow additional spaces in the menu for students to insert additional choices as they come to mind. Ideally, each writer's menu should be individualized to reflect the choices he or she usually makes, as well as several options under each heading that the writer is willing to try out.

**SUGGESTED GROUPING:** individual or pairs

**HOW TO INTRODUCE THE ACTIVITY (SAY/DO):** "Sometimes, as I read students' writing, I hear a small voice in the back of my head going 'bitit,' 'bitit' (sort of like the more familiar frog's 'ribbit, ribbit'). What's that sound?" (Elicit ideas, then continue...) "In fact, it's the sound of BTDT—been there, done that. Too often, students are not venturing into new territory as they develop their talents as writers."

Ask students to take a few moments to peruse their portfolios or writing folders (if these are maintained) or, alternatively, to reflect on the sorts of writing they've done when they weren't assigned a particular topic or form. Have them make a tally mark on the matrix to show the choices they made. Students might wish to work with a partner to confirm the identification of choices from a reader's perspective.

**HOW TO DO THE ACTIVITY:** Pose the choice challenge: Over the course of the next few months (or the rest of the school year), students will periodically have the opportunity to choose the topic, purpose, audience, and form, of the writing they do. Doing so will be like picking a set of choices from a restaurant menu—one from column A (topic), one from column B (audience) and so on. There will be only one constraint. Each piece of writing, when charted on the menu, should be different in some way. Students might wish to venture even further into experimentation, by varying more than one aspect of their work, but minimally, must try at least one new choice.

Some students may be comfortable making decisions about topic, audience, purpose, form, and style/tone as they draft their writing. Others may be more comfortable having a plan ahead of time. For those students, we suggest student-teacher or peer conferencing to identify up front four to six different combinations, which can be charted on the matrix in different colors. As students experiment with each of these choices, they can mark the matrix with BTDT ("been there/done that").

# WRITING CHOICES MENU

| Topic | Audience | Style/Tone | Form |
|---|---|---|---|
| friends | a friend (friends) | funny | story |
| family | classmates | serious | essay |
| animals/nature | other students/peers | thoughtful | letter |
| fantasy | teacher | ironic/sarcastic | report |
| horror | parent(s) | happy | poem |
| history | other familiar adult | uncertain/puzzled | display text |
| school | unfamiliar audience | angry | autobiography |
| _____ | _____ | _____ | _____ |
| _____ | _____ | _____ | _____ |
| _____ | _____ | _____ | _____ |
| _____ | _____ | _____ | _____ |
| _____ | _____ | _____ | _____ |

# VARIATIONS/EXTENSIONS:
# SOME SUGGESTIONS

♦ The notion of an individualized writer's "menu" was first triggered by a chart which was intended to guide the selection of entries in Vermont's portfolio-based writing assessment. You may wish to use the menu, in turn, to establish some parameters for a classroom portfolio system. Create (by yourself, with colleagues, and/or with your students) a menu that captures a rich range and variety of writing tasks. The guidelines for assembling a portfolio can then be described in terms of the menu. Students would be able to choose the selections they wish to include, within certain constraints: for example, writing in at least three content areas must be represented, with no more than two samples from any area; all three purposes for writing (to inform, to persuade, to express personal ideas) must be represented; the intended audience must include both familiar and non-familiar audiences, peers, and adults; at least one piece must include a numeric or graphic component.

♦ Writing-choice menus encourage risk-taking by expanding students' repertoires as writers; menus may encourage a different sort of risk-taking when used for going deeper rather than wider. Some of your students may enjoy the challenge of selecting a choice in one column (for example, one choice of topic, such as sports) and then trying to compose a piece about this topic by utilizing every option from another column (e.g., style/tone) from the menu. Just imagine the possibilities: a serious essay about sports injuries, a humorous story about a particular sports event, an ironic account of one coach's attempt to get a team to "shape up," an objective account of a training regimen, a biting indictment of the impact of Title IX regulations on certain Olympic sports.

♦ This same strategy—pinning down one choice and then exploring the almost limitless possibilities of another—is a very effective way to develop students' sense of attention to audience. For this purpose, have students pick one topic (an issue or event works well) and then craft several versions, each intended for a different audience (a close friend, a group of peers, a teacher or school administrator, parents, a member of the state legislature).

# A True Story

About ten years ago, Gail's younger son Justin was in a rut—he liked to write, but much like the young boys Simmons (1997) describes, everything he wrote was basically a variation on a theme: a scary story about fantastic events, written in a humorous tone, intended to entertain and "gross out" his peers. The "charting writing choices" activity was Gail's response, as both a parent and teacher, to this rut. Parent and child brainstormed and arrived at some other variations in topic, purpose, form, audience, and style or tone, and Gail was the one to pose the challenge: With each subsequent open-ended writing assignment he was given, her son had to change just one thing.

For Justin, topic was the first thing to change. He ventured from criminal adventure into science fiction, and then to more realistic events and everyday occurrences. He more reluctantly experimented with tone, relinquishing his comedian's voice for a more serious one. The last element to change was audience, since his peers were the favored recipients of his craft. Today, a college student and published creative writer, he is still experimenting with choices in writing.

# 16

# AUTHOR'S CRAFT AND THE MAKING OF MEANING: USING TEXT FEATURES IN WRITING

When children are first taught to read, one of the first skills they must acquire is the ability to track words from left to right in order to construct meaning from linear text. As students advance through elementary school and beyond, most explicit instruction in reading and writing continues to focus on traditional, linear text. By the intermediate grades, however, literacy can no longer presume linearity (Hammerberg, 2001). The formats of many textbooks, magazines, manuals, and Web sites offer multiple entrances and exits for the eye and imagination and require understanding of, and facility with, complex text format and a variety of text features.

Given our awareness that boys, as readers, tend to prefer and become most engaged by texts that are visually mediated and crafted—that is, rich in text features that break the linearity of text and contribute to the making of meaning—it makes sense for us to consider instructional strategies that focus on alternative, visually rich ways of crafting text when writing, as well. Both as readers and as writers, boys often respond positively to questions about *how* meaning is made and to investigations of the different ways that a text can be "put together." Boys and girls alike can benefit from opportunities to learn from, and draw on, the kinds of hypertext that they encounter with increasing frequency as readers to develop new approaches to writing for a variety of purposes. "Cut Up Collages" and the activities that follow it address all three purposes for writing and enhance students' facility with creating texts that are multidimensional artifacts that simultaneously bring pleasure and enable students to discover and present what they know in innovative and challenging ways.

# CUT-UP COLLAGES:
# WRITING TO INFORM

One popular reading resource in our instructional community is "Shortcuts," a pullout poster in a weekly "Just for Kids" section of the *Baltimore Sun*. Each week, author-artist Jeff Harris selects a topic of interest to students (and, to teachers' pleasure, well-aligned with their curriculum) such as glaciers, amphibians, germs, or clouds. Unlike another selection that appears each week in the same section called "Story Time"—a traditional story selection comprised of a linearly formatted text accompanied by a facing, full-page illustration—these posters present rich and complex collections of facts, examples, anecdotes, and topical jokes, all interspersed with cartoon-like illustrations (see Figure 16.1 ).They are an example of an increasingly popular "hypertext" genre that, by offering facts, puzzles and testimonies, offers readers multiple opportunities to enter and reenter the text. Although the text is nonlinear, it is not without plan or logic. Instead of organizing information solely by familiar topics (e.g., for an animal, its habitat, diet, reproduction, and adaptations) it also organizes information by type—surprising statistics, corrections to common misconceptions, and "fun facts," for example—and thereby activates such reading skills as determining the schema for the different levels of information and the relationships among them.

Children's responses to these two selections—"Shortcuts" and "Storytime"—exemplify our observations that girls tend to read to fill in (and prefer traditional, linear text forms) and boys tend to read to find out (and prefer visually rich texts). The more traditional ways that teachers often present writing to inform, by having students first read to be informed and then create linear texts in the form of reports, may be limiting both boys' and girls' ways of making meaning as writers. We have discovered, on multiple occasions, that when students are exposed to a nonlinear text and asked to determine the schema which underlie the presentation of information, boys are quicker than girls to figure out the plan. The cut-up collage activity appeals to boys because it activates reading skills at which they excel. At the same time, it encourages girls in their roles as both readers and writers to sharpen their skills at constructing meaning by considering author's craft.

HOW TO GET READY: Based on your curriculum, identify an opportunity for students to do some in-depth reading to be informed about a topic. If possible, students should have the opportunity to choose either a general topic or a specific focus. Thus, for example, in a unit on deserts (or the tropical region), students might choose to focus on land forms, animal life, plant life, or even a particular species. Using a variety of sources (print material such as books, magazines, pamphlets, electronic sources such as Web sites and E-encyclopedias, and media sources such as television and video), students should have the opportunity to gather information on a topic.

You will need to have on hand the following items: large (at least 11" x 17") construction paper or poster board, glue (bottled or gluestick), scissors, markers or colored pencils, and lightweight paper in assorted colors.

SUGGESTED GROUPING: whole class, small group or pair, individual

Figure 16.1 The complex text format and rich array of text features in this poster shape reader's making of meaning.

©Jeff Harris, distributed by United Media (www.comics.com/shortcuts or 800-221-4816).

**HOW TO INTRODUCE THE ACTIVITY (SAY/DO):** "Over the course of the past few [days/weeks], you've been gathering information about _____ (general unit topic). Let's take a few minutes to share some of the things we've learned. What are some particularly interesting or surprising facts, examples, or connections you've come across? What are some things you used to think that you now know are not true?" (Give students an opportunity to review their notes and identify and share some of the things they've learned. Record these, in abbreviated form if necessary, on flip chart paper or the chalkboard.)

"Although the information you've shared is quite varied, it seems to me that you could group the types of information you've shared into several categories. What are some of these?" (Elicit ideas, which might include: general statements, specific facts, comparisons or relationships, examples, personal anecdotes, definitions, misconceptions, and humorous or unusual "believe-it-or-not" asides. If any of these are not proposed by the students, suggest and give an example).

"Sometimes even the most interesting information gets lost on the page because of the way it is presented. Pages after pages of written text, without illustrations, maps, captions, or inserts, can be tedious. To better engage your readers (identify these as either classmates, other students in the school, or another specific audience) in your topic, we're going to explore another format for writing to inform—cut-up collages."

**HOW TO DO THE ACTIVITY:** Share with students a sample cut-up collage or other text in which information is presented in a collage-like fashion, with general categories or types of information signaled through particular borders, colors, or placement. Then, have students work alone, in pairs, or in small groups, to consider some possible ways to use symbols, colors, shapes, or even textures to signal the various types of information they wish to share about the topic they have chosen. For example, they might decide to arrange the collage of information as follows:

| | |
|---|---|
| Broad statements of fact: | Framed boxes |
| Specific, striking details: | Arrow shapes |
| Examples: | Variously shaped inserts in the same color |
| Narrative/Anecdotal asides: | Talk-balloon shapes |
| Humorous Tidbits: | Amoeba shapes in the same color (different color than examples, above) |

Students may also wish to add symbols, images (pictures, diagrams, maps, photographs, etc.) and "engagement activities" (riddles, word searches, or picture searches, for example). Often students will use motifs particular to their topics (e.g., rain forest foliage and bat wings) as symbols and icons. Some may even wish to add interactive elements for their readers such as lift-up flaps or moveable parts (see Figure 16.2).

*Figure 16.2 Students create their own collage posters
on a variety of topics in the science curriculum.*

Give students ample opportunity to share their tentative plans with peers and to revise their collage plan based on feedback. The actual composition and construction may take place in class or as an outside activity.

You can support the reading-writing connection by displaying the completed cut-up collages and inviting peer reviewers to see if they can determine the organizational plan underlying each display of information. Through this step, students have the opportunity to practice drawing inferences based on text features.

# I SEE WHAT YOU MEAN: USING TEXT FEATURES WHEN WRITING POETRY

Because we associate it with introspection and the evocation of emotion, poetry might be the last thing many teachers would think of as an expressive writing activity that would engage the interests of boys as well as girls. However, precisely because author's craft is such an important part of writing poems—attending not only to what meaning is being made but how it is being made as well—boys and girls alike can be easily drawn into poetry writing. Emphasizing the visual and kinetic elements of poetry can be especially rewarding to otherwise reluctant writers. Some ways you might do this include the following:

## Revising/Re-Visioning Poems

At some point after your students have written poems, perhaps in response to a typical prompt or writing exercise, take a few of their samples and reformat them to model the ways that varying text features such as fonts, text size, shape of words, lines or whole poems, and the direction or spacing of letters and words can dramatize meaning and enhance expression. Invite students to compare and remark upon the effects of the revisions that are modeled. Then follow with a guided or collaborative experience, being sure to unpack out loud the thinking behind revisions. You may choose to have each student return to his or her original poem and revise it to increase richness of text features, or simply have students add these strategies to their internal "tool box" to use at some point in the future (see Figure 16.3).

## Acclaim for Frames

As long as there has been poetry, poets have made use of established forms or frames to structure their ideas and feelings. While most elementary and middle school teachers avoid traditional forms such as the sonnet or sestina, finding these too demanding for their students, it is common to see in classrooms such forms as haiku, cinquain, and list poems. The possibilities for forms and frames is endless, however, and the ability to recognize the underlying structure of a poem and to imitate that structure serves students well when the time comes to write poetry.

## Rumbling Thunder!

Thunder makes me feel scared it's very loud and comes with big black clouds. A lot of times lightning follows the thunder and goes flash flash and takes the electricity out And thunder goes boooooooooom booooooooom. It feels like a earthquake shaking the ground an house and rattling the dishes and windows. That's why rumbling thunder scares me.

---

Rumbling Thunder!

Thunder makes me feel scared.
It's very LOUD
and comes with **big black clouds**.
A lot of times
Lightning follows the thunder and goes

flash, flash

and takes the electricity out.
And thunder goes
boooooooooom!
boooooooooooooom!
It feels like an earthquake
shaking the ground
and house
and
r-a-t-t-l-l-n-g
the dishes and windows.
That's why
**rumbling thunder**
scares me.

*Figure 16.3 Text features such as font variation and line length enhance the visual and dramatic impact of this student's poem about thunder.*

You have only to look at one poem we discovered when examining student responses from a statewide assessment (see Figure 16.4). Even the time constraints and somewhat sterile conditions of a standardized test couldn't keep this poet down.

The Cat

Watch the cat sit,
Hear the cat purr.
Smell him as he walks past you,
Feel him as he rubs against you with his fur.
Oh, the cat.

See his hairballs.
He feels like silk.
Hear him as he falls.
He smells like cat litter.
Oh, the cat.

See his scratch marks in the chairs,
Hear him when he gets hurt.
Feel him when you pet him but watch
out for his tiny hairs.
Smell him, he smells like wet grass.
Oh, the cat.

*Figure 16.4 This young poet uses a particular stanzaic form, beginning each line with a sense word and ending with a refrain, to frame a poem.*

What jumps out immediately when reading "The Cat" is that the young writer didn't start from scratch. Familiarity with a frame permitted this student to craft an engaging poem. Without knowing for certain, we think it's likely that this student was lucky enough to have one or more teachers who took the time, when reading poetry with students, to ask, "What do you notice about this poem?" and to share observations about such framing devices as rhyme, rhetorical features, repetition, and counts. Opportunities to move from "now you see" to "now you do" using a variety of frames expands students' "toolbox" to which they may return whenever they have the occasion to write to express personal ideas.

## Step by Step with Frames

At any point when you are sharing a poem which demonstrates an underlying shape or structure:

♦ *Discover the frame* (lead students to recognize the presence of a frame).

♦ *Uncover the frame* (provide or collaborate with students to capture the essential elements of the frame).

- *Fill the frame* (craft a new poem using the elements you've identified).

When reading Ivy Eastwick's poem, "Thanksgiving," for example, students were guided to notice, among other features, stanzas of eight lines, shaped along a diagonal. They noticed that the first line of each stanza is the same and that each stanza focuses a different sense with examples of things that can be touched, seen, and heard. For our own thanksgiving poems, we decided to change the stanza shape, but keep the same first line. Students chose the order in which they wished to present the senses, and were invited to add or change senses (taste and smell being an important part of the Thanksgiving experience, after all!). Using the basic frame identified, students each wrote their own "Poem of Thanks." Results were quite varied, original, and uniformly successful (see Figure 16.5).

# A COMIC CONFLICT: USING TEXT FEATURES TO ENHANCE PERSUASIVE WRITING

Reluctant writers who struggle to fill the page when writing a persuasive essay or letter may respond positively to the opportunity to develop arguments and counterarguments in comic-strip form. Doing so engages students' familiarity with a popular genre and offers a form in which arguments may be distilled to their essence. The jumping-off point for this activity is identifying an issue, problem, or decision about which students want others to think or act a certain way. Have students brainstorm about possible topics ranging from personal and school issues to more public ones; some examples they might come up with are:

- I (older children) shouldn't have to babysit for my siblings
- I (middle schoolers) shouldn't have a curfew
- I (our class) shouldn't have to write in a reading log every day
- Teen drivers shouldn't have a probationary year
- Students shouldn't be required to perform community service

Have students each select one issue, and then decide upon two characters they think would be convincing spokespersons for opposing sides of the issue. Students should then draw a representation (the more highly stylized, the better) of each character with a talk balloon issuing from his or her mouth (or their mouths, if either or both sides represent a group). In preparation, you may wish to discuss the ways that cartoonists use, and usually exaggerate, one or two features to signal personality or attitude. Then, make five or six photocopies of each student's set of pictures that can then be ordered sequentially to create a complete comic strip.

Through brief discussion, elicit students' recollections about characteristics of persuasive writing. In particular, make sure students understand that persuasive writing makes clear the writer's position towards an issue, problem, or decision, and provides developed reasons to support that position, along with ideas or examples to refute the claims of the opposition.

**Thanksgiving**

Thank You
for all my hands can hold—
apples, red,
and melons gold,
yellow corn
both ripe and sweet,
peas and beans
so good to eat!

Thank You
for all my eyes can see—
lovely sunlight,
field and tree,
white cloud-boats
in sea-deep sky,
soaring bird
and butterfly.

Thank You
for all my ears can hear—
birds' song echoing
far and near,
songs of little
stream, big sea,
cricket, bullfrog,
duck and bee!

**A Poem of Thanks**

Thank you
For all my ears can hear—

-ear

X

X

Thank you
For all my eyes can see—

-ee

X

X

Thank you
For all my hands can hold—

-old

X

**A Poem of Thanks**

Thank you
For all my ears can hear—
Children's laughter
Birds' song clear
Drums and trumpets
Festive cheers
All are music
To my ears

Thank you
For all my eyes can see—
In my mirror
A reflection of me
Flowers blooming
In every hue
Sun, moon, stars
shadows, smiles and you

Thank you
For all my hands can hold—
Puppies warm
And snowballs cold
A bat and ball
A leather glove
The hand of someone
Else I love

*Figure 16.5 Students discover, uncover and fill in a poetry frame.*

("Thanksgiving" from *Cherry Stones! Garden Swings!* [1963] used by permission of Abingdon Press.)

Either individually or in pairs, students will use their cartoon boxes to set forth their position, reasons, and counterarguments. Once the panels are drafted, have each student (or pair of students) decide upon a preferred order for the cartoon picture panels. Classmates may be consulted to confirm or revise the order of picture panels, and then the panels should be taped together into a long cartoon strip. As an alternative, students can use 3" x 5" cards and draw freehand the cartoon characters and talk balloons on each, before ordering and taping together the sequence.

In the spirit of cartoons and comics, logic need not win over passion; after a detailed and clearly youth-oriented argument is rejected by the opposing character or characters—a teacher, principal, or parents, for example—the "last word" can be added to the mouth of the student or his or her surrogate.

# 17

# SELLING/ DISPELLING GENDER STEREOTYPES

When we write to persuade, our goal is to get someone else to think or act in a particular way. Effective persuasion requires careful analysis of the rhetorical situation (purpose, audience, etc.); assessment of audience concerns, needs and beliefs; facility with a range of appeals (to readers' beliefs, logic, emotions, and values); establishment of credibility; and acknowledgment and refutation of alternative interpretations, choices, or points of view. Our research showed that boys and girls tend to approach persuasive tasks somewhat differently. Boys tend to focus on general advantages or disadvantages of a given action or position, rather than on the impact that taking such an action would have or the possible repercussions of that position. They seem less attentive to the particulars of a rhetorical situation and the ways that the needs and perspectives of their audience can be used to shape their message. Girls are more likely to accurately analyze the complexity of the rhetorical situation, to orient their texts toward their intended readers, to draw on a range of appeals, and to acknowledge alternative points of view. At times, however, their attention to the relationships implied in a hypothetical situation seems to distract them from marshaling information and drawing on appropriate knowledge bases. We found that refuting alternative points of view was challenging for both boys and girls.

Because advertisements are the most accessible, familiar, and concentrated examples of persuasion in our culture, they provide an excellent opportunity to strengthen students' abilities both to analyze and to construct persuasive texts. The following activity will both enhance students' awareness of the audience- and purpose-driven choices writers make and enable them to exercise some of those choices in their own writing. Advertisements also offer fertile ground to consider one powerful way that gender is defined and shaped in our culture. Just as greater attention to gender issues enables teachers to consider texts in new ways, so, too, our students can benefit from analysis of the ways gender is constructed in the words and the worlds around them.

# ANALYZING ADS

**HOW TO GET READY:** If your class has not already discussed stereotypes in another context, this is an ideal moment to engage students in a discussion of what stereotypes are and why they can be harmful. Students as young as third grade are usually easily able to identify stereotypes they have encountered among peers, in popular media, and in their own experience.

In preparation for this assignment, you might also have students brainstorm to make a list of strategies and appeals they would use to persuade their parents to allow them to do something or purchase something they want. With students, classify these strategies using a kid-friendly and age appropriate version of Aristotle's analysis of persuasion from over 2000 years ago. For each argument given, determine whether the appeal is to:

♦ logic and fact (*logos*)—statistics, scientific evidence, or data (*e.g., I need a palm pilot because studies show that students who use them get higher SAT scores*)

♦ emotions, fears and desires (*pathos*)—flattery, exaggeration of an anxiety, or jealousy (*e.g., I just don't know how I'll be able to keep track of deadlines and appointments without a palm pilot*)

♦ values and beliefs or the authority of the speaker (*ethos*)—establishment of the persuader as reasonable, informed and ethical (*e.g., a recent study by NCTE called for equity in availability of all electronic learning tools, which would include not only graphing calculators but also palm pilots*)

♦ a combination of these strategies

Choose an advertisement from the early years of this century. An excellent source is Ad*Access (http://scriptorium.lib.duke.edu/adaccess/), an educational web site that makes accessible over 7000 advertisements from the last hundred years. We have found that an historical advertisement adds a touch of humor, and also makes it easier for students to identify the often dated or exaggerated cultural assumptions embedded in an advertisement.

Engage students in a discussion of such questions as:

♦ What is the purpose of the advertisement?

♦ What product is being promoted?

♦ On what basis does the advertisement seek to persuade the audience?

♦ To what emotions does the advertisement appeal—A fear of rejection? A desire to be popular or loved? Anxiety about one's appearance?

♦ In what ways is the advertisement tailored to a particular audience?

♦ How does the advertisement establish credibility or authority? What have the advertisers done to make the claims in the advertisement believable (use of a celebrity, inclusion of facts or statistics)?

♦ What is the relationship between the image and the words in this advertisement? What associations does the image create with the product being promoted?

♦ What stereotypes does the advertisement reinforce or challenge?

♦ What is assumed or implied about the world, and specifically about the roles and attitudes of women or men? What seems to be assumed about women and men in the working world, at home, or in relationship to each other? Would the ad work if the gender of the person in the ad were changed? Why or why not?

This discussion will prepare students for engaging in their own analyses of more recent ads.

**SUGGESTED GROUPING:** individual

**HOW TO INTRODUCE THE ACTIVITY (SAY/DO):** Ask students to look through any magazines they may have at home or to choose one of several you have collected and have on hand in the classroom. Each student should choose two advertisements to analyze: one that portrays what they believe are negative or stereotypical gender roles, and one that they believe offers more varied or positive images.

**HOW TO DO THE ACTIVITY:** Distribute two copies of the "Advertisement Review Form" (see page 146) to each student. Have students will fill out the analysis sheet for each advertisement and use that information, along with the advertisements themselves, to give a brief oral presentation to their classmates.

Then, following these presentations, students will use the persuasive techniques that the class has discussed to create an advertisement of their own. This might be for a real product currently on the market, for an imaginary product, or for an issue or cause of interest to them. To help students understand this last category of advertisement, you may wish to share some examples of public service announcements or advertisements. Samples of these are available through the Ad Council (www.adcouncil.org), an organization that creates public service announcements promoting education, health, fairness and environmental awareness. Based on your students' interests and the connections you hope to make to the curriculum, you may wish to encourage them to research, and become more informed about, the issue they've chosen, in order to get beyond cliche and incorporate a fuller range of evidence.

# VARIATIONS/EXTENSIONS: SOME SUGGESTIONS

♦ Students can use the "advertisement review form" to analyze their own advertisement. This analysis may take the form of a one-paragraph statement explaining the rationale for the choices they made, the images they have presented, and the persuasive techniques they used.

♦ As an alternative, while still at draft stage, students can exchange their advertisements with a classmate, and analyze each other's ads using the "advertisement review form." This form of focused peer review will call attention to each student's use of persuasive techniques and to other techniques the student may incorporate.

# ADVERTISEMENT REVIEW FORM

Who is the intended audience for this advertisement? How is that made clear?

_____

_____

_____

What product, idea, or action is being promoted in this advertisement?

_____

_____

_____

How does the advertisement seek to persuade the audience?
(To what emotions does the ad appeal? What makes the advertisement believable?)

_____

_____

_____

In what ways is the advertisement tailored to a particular audience?

_____

_____

_____

What is the relationship between the images and the words in this advertisement?
What do the images suggest about the product being promoted?

_____

_____

_____

What stereotypes does the advertisement reinforce or challenge? How?

_____

_____

_____

# 18
# WRITING AS AN AGGRESSIVE/ TRANSGRESSIVE ACT

Even though most students are on "best behavior" when writing for large-scale assessments, from our years of experience reading test responses we recall memorable exceptions, including the ones that follow. In response to a prompt to write about a school improvement, one student suggested that students and administrators establish a "teacher torture room"; in response to directions to write an advertisement for a service teens might offer, another student offered a jaunty ad for "PetKillers" to ensure neighborhood quiet and cleanliness; and in response to an open-ended prompt to write a story, poem, or play about a topic of the students' choice, we saw a plethora of poems on the order of the following:

The state test

Is an awful tragedy

Third and fifth grades take it

And they both hate it

The only people who like it are eggheads though

To all the other people it's their worst foe

I'm taking the state test and I hate it a lot

I'd rather be left in a dumpster to rot

Few of us would be surprised to learn that this heartfelt verse was written by a boy. In fact, the desire to adopt an oppositional or ironic stance and to challenge authority was one of the striking characteristics we noted in boys' writing, particularly the writing of middle schoolers. This kind of "writing with an attitude" usually precipitates mixed reactions from teachers, who may be at once disturbed by the anger or violence in these pieces and yet appreciative of the irreverent humor and *Monty Python/Saturday Night Live* artfulness that they possess. Recognizing that many of the narratives children encounter daily are similarly filled with exaggerated violence, some teachers may ask whether creating opportunities for writing like this can provide a legitimate channel for engagement with, and transformation and mediation of, the "underlife" that always bubbles below the official classroom curriculum but is only rarely allowed to surface as potentially meaningful material to support school literacy.

In this post-Columbine era, educators may react to students' transgressive and often violent writing with greater unease than ever before, alarmed at some writers' endorsement of violence to resolve conflict, lack of empathy for victims of violence, and subordination of entire groups of people. One response on teachers' part is to actively suppress writing that expresses feelings of hostility or negativism. With the greatest respect for the need for educators to be vigilant, and to recognize the cries for help often left by children, particularly adolescents, in a writer's journal or the seemingly anonymous pages of a test booklet, the "transgressive" topic choices and development strategies of many boys as writers may call for some alternatives to alarm or censorship. These alternatives incorporate material from popular culture that engages so many students, invite the kinds of play, performance, and competition that characterizes meaningful peer relationships, and permit students to shed a compliant posture. In proposing these alternatives, we join a growing number of educators such as Anne Haas Dyson (1997), Mary Hilton (1996), Thomas Newkirk (2000), and Jeffrey Wilhelm (1997) who advocate making the boundaries between school literacy and peer and popular culture more permeable. Assuming that print literacy can be made more attractive and possible by being embedded in narrative styles that are familiar to students from popular culture, the following activities create legitimate opportunities for students to adopt transgressive stances. They acknowledge the propensity of some students to compose intense, action-packed and conflict-ridden stories which demand attention to motive and emotion, and others to write stories that can be enlivened by heightened action and drama.

# ACTION/REACTION

**HOW TO GET READY:** Either on your own or with the help of your students, select a brief video clip that depicts a physical conflict. Martial arts films, animation featuring superheroes and villains, and films depicting wars of past or future are all useful sources of such clips.

**SUGGESTED GROUPING:** Small groups—representing video "production teams"—assigned or established as follows:

- One student for each character represented in the video clip

- One student to serve as "director"

- Any extra students may join or be assigned to a "production team" as an extra cast member (e.g., a narrator) or scenery or makeup coordinator

Depending on your students' familiarity with the characteristics of dramatic text forms (skits, plays, scenes, radio plays, etc.), you may wish to introduce a mini-lesson at this point on the text features unique to drama using "Key Text Features of Dramatic Forms" as a resource.

# Key Text Features of Dramatic Forms

**Headings**—In some ways, plays are formatted like "Reading to Perform a Task" selections: They may identify, up front, what is needed to perform the play. So, for example, the text may include such headings (followed by relevant information) as characters, setting, play length, props, and costumes. If the play is comprised of more than one act, the text will most likely include headings that identify each act, sometimes followed by a brief description of setting (e.g., winter, near Valley Forge, 1777).

**Speaking Parts**—Plays identify the speaker of each line or running set of lines. Generally, the speaker's name or role is given in bold face or a distinctive font, followed by a colon. For example:

DETECTIVE:　　　Snow White:　　　***Farmers:***

**Parenthetical Directions**—Sometimes, between the identification of the speaker(s) and the actual lines, readers will see some parenthetical information. This may include;

- ◆ manner of oral delivery　(whispering) (shouts) (angrily)
- ◆ manner of expression　　(looks horrified) (pleased with himself)
- ◆ action　　　　　　　　(pointing) (bending) (kneeling at the base of the statue)
- ◆ direction　　　　　　　(entering stage right) (facing stage rear) (to audience)
- ◆ order　　　　　　　　(in turns) (together)

**Play Talk**—When reading, writing, and/or talking about plays and the texts of plays, certain words are frequently used:

- ◆ script:　the written text of the play
- ◆ part:　the character or role that someone is performing
- ◆ props:　the objects that are used to help identify characters and setting, or to create an effect
- ◆ act:　parts into which a longer play may be divided—acts usually change to denote a different time or place
- ◆ scene:　like acts, these are parts of a play—often dividing an act to denote a change in time or place
- ◆ stage:　the area in which the performance takes place; it may be in front of or in the middle of the area where the audience assembles
- ◆ ad-lib:　making up a line or an action that is not in the script but makes sense in the scene

**Stage Directions**—Some scripts refer to various parts of the stage, so everyone will know where characters and props are supposed to be located

| upstage right | upstage center | upstage left |
|---|---|---|
| stage right | center stage | stage left |
| downstage right | downstage center | downstage left |

From *Reading, Writing, and Gender* by Goldberg and Roswell (© 2002).
Permission to duplicate for classroom use is granted by Eye On Education, Larchmont, NY.

**HOW TO INTRODUCE THE ACTIVITY (SAY/DO):** "Think about a time when you have watched a particularly violent film in the movies or on television." (Pause to allow students some time to think, and then continue...) "Take a few moments to consider:

- "What happened during one event involving conflict?

- "Why did the violence occur?

- "How did those involved feel about it?

- "What was the outcome of the event—not just physically, but emotionally—for those involved?"

Through discussion, elicit from students their awareness that in most, if not all, instances, it was unlikely that they knew about the causes and consequences of conflict. There was lots of action, but little evidence of reaction.

"Creating an action sequence requires the work of a whole crew—actors, writers, directors, and specialists in scenery and makeup. Today, you're going to create another 'take' or version of an action sequence—one that adds some of the emotions and effects that many of you found missing from action sequences you've seen."

**HOW TO DO THE ACTIVITY:** Play the video clip you've selected. At this point, either assign roles or invite students to form groups as "production crews." Given the series of actions that comprise the event they've witnessed, students should decide:

- why the event occurred (problem/solution)

- how those involved (on and off the actual scene) felt before, during, and after the actions that students witnessed

- what the consequences (both physically and emotionally) of those actions were

Students should collaborate to create a revised script for the episode. Their challenge is to create—through such means as asides, dialogue, narrator's voice for introduction and/or epilogue, as well as through descriptions of costume and setting through parenthetical directions—a richer sense of the emotions behind the event (see Figure 18.1). The product that students create may take several forms, ranging from the text alone to students' performance of a "voice over" of the episode. Actual performances are to be discouraged, for obvious reasons!

# VARIATIONS/EXTENSIONS: SOME SUGGESTIONS

- As an extra challenge, you may wish to play the video clip on "mute" and invite students to create all dialogue from scratch. These "silent movies" permit students to rethink the ways that violence is typically represented in martial arts and war movies, with the not uncommon outcome that they override the inherent and often gratuitous violence with humor.

# Sample Student Video Scripts

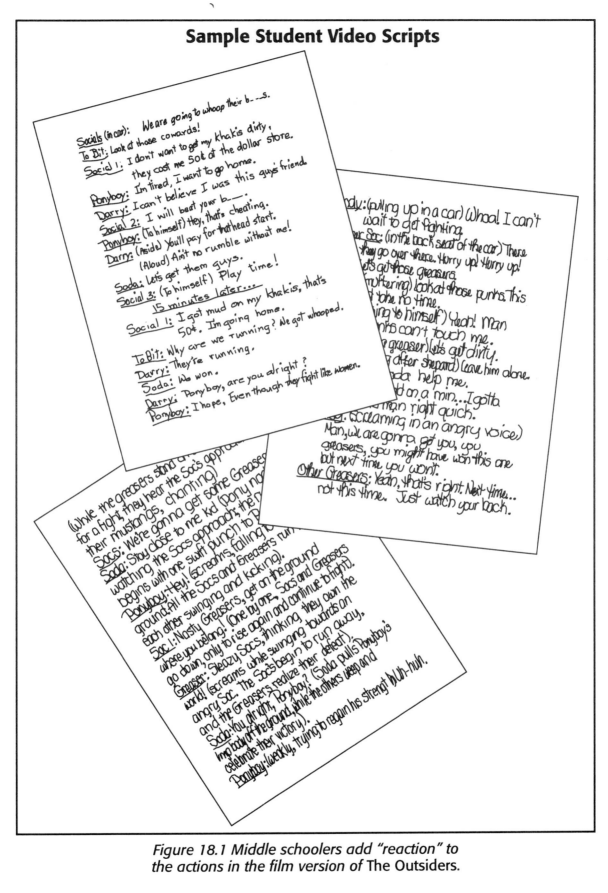

*Figure 18.1 Middle schoolers add "reaction" to
the actions in the film version of* The Outsiders.

- Another alternative is to use video games instead of films (animated or otherwise). Again, the redundancy of knock-down, drag-out fights and often graphic displays of violence can be creatively tempered with description, dialogue, and reflection that infuses context into conflict.

- Comic books offer yet another vehicle for revisiting action-oriented narrative episodes and infusing them with greater context. In preparation, obtain one or more comic books featuring action-packed and violence-prone sequences. Use cut-and-paste shapes or white-out to cover up the contents of talk balloons (and thought balloons, as well, if any appear). Students will work individually or in pairs to create dialogue for the comic characters that is richer than usual in references to feelings, impressions, and reflection. Especially if the cartoon contains few thought balloons—or none at all—encourage students to add this text feature to give readers a better sense of the thoughts and feelings behind each character's actions.

# 19
# RETELLING COUNTS

When students have the opportunity to choose what they write, more than a few—and more boys than girls—will choose to retell an existing story, either satirizing a familiar tale, creating a sequel to or variation on a favorite story, film, or television program, or reworking characters, plots devices and story lines to create a "twist" on a known text. Such stories are sometimes devalued in classroom and assessment contexts, because of the premium that we tend to put on originality. While originality is indeed to be prized, research tells us that children typically explore narrative forms and learn to become proficient writers through imitation and modeling. Moreover, classrooms in which peer response and sharing are the norm, imitation of peers' work, often itself derivative, is a key aspect of collaboration (Freedman, 1995; Simmons, 1997). Anne Haas Dyson's many books and articles argue convincingly for the pleasure and power emerging writers experience as they create retellings to "master" familiar genres, make the materials their own, and connect with peers who share their interests. Even writers older than those Dyson generally observes can benefit from opportunities to revisit and retell familiar texts. Peter Thomas, noting that "boys tend to be more confident in reproducing a genre; girls in adapting it," regards mimesis, if controlled and purposeful, as an important strategy for intermediate writers (1997, p. 30). Jeffrey Wilhelm (1997), who works with adolescents, endorses writing activities that enable reluctant readers to "be the book" and to reexperience narratives from the "inside out." The following activities transform retelling from a sporadic, and even discounted, event on the periphery of writing instruction into a legitimate, and even celebrated, route into expressive writing.

## OFT-TOLD TALES

**HOW TO GET READY:** Select a familiar story and at least one retelling or alternative version of that story. One possible set of retellings for intermediate students is:

- *The Three Little Pigs* (original folktale)
- *The True Story of the Three Little Pigs* (John Scieszka)
- *The Three Little Javelinas* (Susan Lowell)
- *The Three Little Wolves and the Big Bad Pig* (Eugene Trivizas)

Middle school students might enjoy the following variations on a theme, which include some "juvenile" retellings as well as several that are more biting and sophisticated:

- *Cinderella* (Brothers Grimm version)

- *Cinder-Elly* (Frances Minters)

- *Ella Enchanted* (Gail Carson Levine)

- "Cinderella" in *Revolting Rhymes* (Roald Dahl)

- "Cinderella," in *Transformations* ( Anne Sexton)

On the chalkboard or a flip chart, create a matrix with rows listing a variety of story elements (e.g., characters/character traits, setting, problem, solution, and main events) and a column for each version of the story students will examine.

Either independently or as a class, read the original and one or more versions of the story. If using more than one alternative version, you may wish to jigsaw readings so that different groups are assigned different selections.

**SUGGESTED GROUPING:** small groups, whole class, then individual

**HOW TO INTRODUCE THE ACTIVITY (SAY/DO):** "Think about the story you just read, and consider ways that it was like and unlike the original version of that story. For example, perhaps the characters were the same, but the traits they displayed were reversed (e.g., there are still three pigs, but in the new version they are bad instead of good, while the wolf is good instead of bad)." (Generate observations about similarities and differences between/among the selections. Encourage students to consider how the retelling may have helped them to see the original in a new way. Did any of the retellings have a "point" or a "moral" different from that of the original? Through discussion, guide students towards recognition that in effective retellings, some elements stay the same, and others change.)

"It is the balance between the familiar and the new twists in these stories that makes such retellings pleasurable for us to read. Today, you'll have the opportunity to write/retell this story or another that is familiar to you and your classmates. When completed, we'll display an array of retellings (outside our classroom, in the library/media center, or another school-based location)."

**HOW TO DO THE ACTIVITY:** To help them with planning, give students a story element graphic organizer on which to record the details of the particular story or fairytale they wish to retell (see page 59 for one example). Students should then determine which element or elements they wish to change, in order to achieve a particular goal for their retelling—to update a story, to call attention to a missing point of view, or to change the perception of a particular character. Be sure to make clear, as students begin to plan their stories, that they, like all writers, are free to alter initial decisions and redirect along the way. Suggest that they start by planning for one or two key differences between their version of the story and the original. Point out that if too many elements are different, then readers may not recognize the "roots" of the story and not appreciate the retelling for what it intends to be. These revisions to the original version should be recorded on the organizer, using another color ink or by crossing out and overlaying new details (see Figure 19.1) that will shape the retelling (see Figure 19.2).

**Story Map**

**Title** The Three Little Pigs

**Setting**

The country     The town

**Characters**

| 3 nice pigs | 3 bad pigs |
| 1 bad wolf | 1 nice wolf |
| | 1 boy |

**Problem**

Pigs need a safe place to live     Boy is annoyed by pigs

Pigs annoy boy

Event 1 ~~Pig builds house of straw. Wolf destroys house and eats pig.~~

Boy gets help from wolf

Event 2 ~~Pig 2 builds house of sticks. Wolf destroys house and eats pig.~~

Wolf eats pig!

Event 3 ~~Pig 3 builds house of bricks. Wolf tries to destroy house but can't.~~

Wolf eats pig 2 ... Wolf eats pig 3

Event 4 ~~Pig 3 tricks Wolf and Wolf dies.~~

Event 5     Pigs and wolf disappear

**Solution**

~~Pig 3 is safe from Wolf in house of bricks.~~     Boy is safe from pigs

### The Wolf who Died

One day three pigs were moving into town where this boy lived, and his name was John. Every day when John went out to play, the pigs chased John across town. John was so mad, he did not know what to do with those pigs. So he thought and thought, and he thought of the wolf who lived down the street.

John went to the wolf's house and asked, "Mr. Wolf, can you eat those pigs who just moved into town?"

"Yes, I will eat those pigs."

So the wolf called the first little pig. "Little pig, can you come to my house and have some ice cream with me?" he asked.

When the pig went to his house, the wolf ate him up in one.

After that, the wolf called the next pig and said, "Little pig, can you come to my house? I'm very sick and I need someone to make some tea."

The pig went over to the wolf's house and the wolf ate the little pig up.

Then the wolf called the next pig and said, "Little pig, I have something for you."

The little pig went to the wolf's house and was eaten all up.

After the wolf ate those pigs, he died the next day. Nobody knows where the pigs are or where the wolf is. Some people say the wolf and pigs are dead. Other people say they are alive. But no one knows for sure.

*Figure 19.2 One student's retelling of the "Three Little Pigs."*

To facilitate students' envisionments of "once told" and retold versions of a familiar tale, you may wish to instruct them to fold the organizer to create two columns for each story element, or use an organizer designed specifically with this activity in mind (see page 158). Once their retellings have been tentatively mapped out, students should begin drafting. The organizer may also serve as a useful aid during peer response and revision, as students consider whether they've changed enough details to "update" the story but not so many that the connection to the original is obscured.

Once these retellings are completed, encourage students to plan a display that includes not only their stories, grouped so that all retellings of the same story appear together, but all published versions they can find (both original and retold) and related artifacts such as stuffed toys, comics or cartoons, video versions, and toys and games.

## VARIATIONS/EXTENSIONS

Once students have some general familiarity with the concept of literary retellings, consider one or more of the following activities:

### From Margin to Center

Some retellings can be considered "innocent" variations on a theme; these stories offer writers the pleasure of building a new story on an existing framework and often enable students, especially younger ones, to stretch beyond what they are able to create with wholly new material. More often, however, and particularly among older students, retellings may be motivated by some desire to reverse a set of roles or power relationships, to challenge the assumptions of a well-known text, or to move a perspective that has been excluded from the margins to the center of a text. Retellings have therefore been a favorite genre of feminist authors and others outside of the "mainstream" who often want to reenter a text through a "backdoor" and voice perspectives that previously had been mute. In recent years, these retellings by marginal characters have become so popular, in fact, that in response to the publication announcement of Alice Randall's *The Wind Done Gone*, a retelling of Margaret Mitchell's *Gone with the Wind* from the perspective of Scarlett's mulatto half sister, the *New York Times* (April 8, 2001) ran a cartoon of yet another retelling: *Gone With Me: As Told by The Wind*.

A powerful reading/writing connection is forged if you invite students to reinvent a story or section of a familiar book with the express intention of "moving the margin to the center." Instead of merely shifting perspective or point of view from a main to a more subsidiary character, as students did in "Rethinking the Story Map," this sort of retelling might involve inventing new but plausible characters and events to give voice to marginalized peoples or perspectives. Students should be encouraged to think about their motivation for their retelling, so that the choices they make contribute to a new vision they want to express.

# Oft-Told Tales

| *As once told* | *As retold* |
|---|---|
| Characters | Characters |
| Setting | Setting |
| Problem | Problem |
| Key Events | Key Events |
| Solution/Resolution | Solution/Resolution |
| Moral or message | Moral or message |

## Retelling as Updating

Updated versions of classics have long been staples in middle school curricula, with the pairing of *Romeo and Juliet* and *West Side Story* a well-established favorite. In another reading/writing connection, students may wish to retell a story by updating it to reflect more contemporary times. In this case, students should be encouraged to think of essential elements of character or plot, and to search for contemporary "touchstones" or emblems of those traits. For example, what details from contemporary life would best represent Cinderella's stepmother's vanity, greed and selfishness? Obsessing over the Home Shopping Network? Engineering "photo-ops" or society-page citations for her own daughters of marriageable age? Guide students to see that vivid, true-to-contemporary life details (talking too loudly on a cell phone in public places, using two spaces to park your SUV, for example) can be used simultaneously to define a character and to comment on the student's own world.

## Ventriloquism

Instead of retelling a familiar story through a new voice, students alternatively can adopt a the voice of a familiar character or author to tell a new, but plausible story. This technique, which can be adapted to nonfiction as well as fictional texts, enables student to "try on" an unfamiliar voice—that speaker's syntax, favored vocabulary, pacing and emphasis, as well as to reflect upon the impact of situation and setting on a given character. Especially when done with a character or author with a very distinctive voice (Cleary's Ramona Quimby, Rowling's Harry Potter, or Lemony Snicket, pseudonymous author of the *A Series of Unfortunate Events* books), this activity is a very effective way for students to get inside another person's way of conceptualizing the world.

## Regenerate a Genre

Students may enjoy playing upon a familiar genre rather than a specific, familiar work of literature or storyline from television or film. Set the stage by generating discussion about the characteristics of a particular genre (horror stories, for example, or mass murderer films like the "Halloween" or "Scream" series). Working within this genre, for example, the young author of "Cereal Killer" (see Figure 19.3) captured the formula of "warning issued/warning ignored" through which victims meet their nemesis, but with an effective twist.

The basic notion of a retelling holds within it a host of variations beyond retelling stories from a different point of view or transforming individual story elements. Many of these activities can be organized for groups, so that students collaborate to create the new text. Students can be encouraged to "open a door" in an existing story, and create a scene that is only implied, to speculate about events occurring before or after the story, or to transform the story into another genre—a newspaper report into a story or poem, a story into the form of a news report or interview; the possibilities are many.

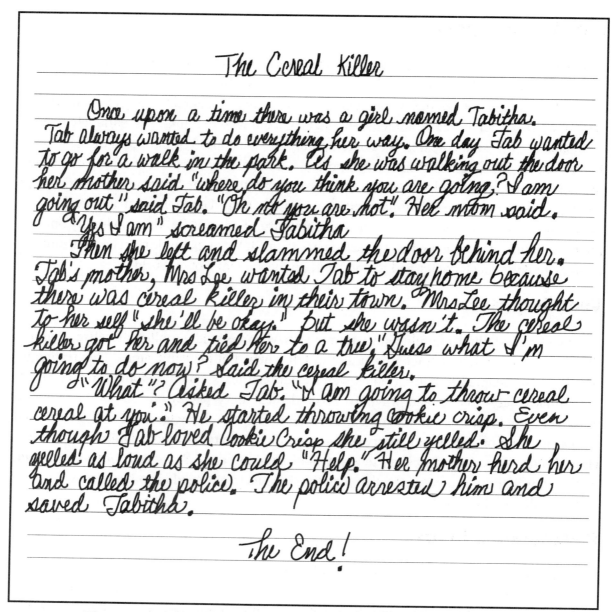

# The Cereal Killer

Once upon a time there was a girl named Tabitha. Tab always wanted to do everything her way. One day Tab wanted to go for a walk in the park. As she was walking out the door her mother said. "where do you think you are going? I am going out" said Tab. "Oh no you are not." Her mom said.

"Yes I am" screamed Tabitha

Then she left and slammed the door behind her. Tab's mother, Mrs Lee wanted Tab to stay home because there was cereal killer in their town. Mrs Lee thought to her self "she'll be okay." but she wasn't. The cereal killer got her and tied her to a tree "Guess what I'm going to do now? Said the cereal killer.

"What"? Asked Tab. "I am going to throw cereal cereal at you." He started throwing cookie crisp. Even though Tab loved Cookie Crisp she still yelled. She yelled as loud as she could "Help." Her mother herd her and called the police. The police arrested him and saved Tabitha.

The End!

Figure 19.3 One student plays with the conventions of horror films.

# 20

# POSTSCRIPT: BEYOND THE PAGE AND BEYOND THESE PAGES

As we did in the preface to this book, once again we invite you to "picture a reader." We hope that the images that now come to mind are rich and varied, peopled with children reading alone and together, enjoying texts of many sorts, thinking about their individual preferences, and talking about and evaluating what they have read with attention to a full range of characters, plots, and emotions. When you picture a writer, we hope you see similar diversity and energy, as children write for a variety of purposes in a variety of forms, experimenting as they do with different ways of developing and organizing what they write, with as much attention to how meaning is made as to what meaning they convey.

Each of the activities described in the pages of this book provides an opportunity to observe how boys and girls use language to make sense of the world—and we hope as you introduce them to your students, you are asking all sorts of questions: Did some activities you tried appeal more to the boys or to the girls in your classroom? Did some create resistance, at least initially, and what meaning do you make of that resistance? Which activities caused students to respond in ways very different from those you might have anticipated? What new ways of thinking and acting as readers and writers have your students internalized and made their own, and how has this affected their work on a broader scale? In what ways did you (or would you now) adapt and revise these activities, and why?

Addressing the ways that boys and girls may be "differently literate" is an endeavor much in need of our collective curiosity, inquiry, and dialogue. We hope that you will share not just these activities and the student work that results from them, but also what you learn from these activities about boys and girls, readers and writers, teaching and learning.

Our experiences with the many instructional strategies and classroom activities we have described suggests that there are no insurmountable barriers to both boys and girls becoming proficient in constructing meaning effectively as readers and as writers. While we don't profess to be able to dramatically change the world in which our students find themselves, we can and must use our growing understanding of gender-specific behaviors and attitudes, temperaments and learning styles, to widen the approaches we take when teaching reading and writing. Curriculum, instruction, and assessment will be more powerful and positive for our efforts to expand and apply that understanding.

# RECOMMENDED READING ON LITERACY AND GENDER

One of our objectives in writing this book was to nurture an ongoing conversation among parents and educators about literacy and gender. If you would like to do some further reading, we recommend the following books and articles which have helped to shape our thinking, and which may also act as catalysts for your future inquiry. Whether you pursue further reading on your own, or with colleagues as part of a book club or school-based seminar, we believe you will find these selected works both thought-provoking and engagingly written.

Alvine, L., & Cullum, L. (1999). *Breaking the cycle: Gender, literacy and learning.* Portsmouth, NH: Boynton/Cook.

> This varied collection of essays focuses primarily on the unique needs and strengths of adolescent girls as readers. Sections of the book (a) address the ways that reading and writing can constrain the development of both boys and girls by reinforcing rather than disrupting stereotypes, (b) offer strategies (including syllabi and assignments) to assist in curriculum transformation, and (c) analyze girls' out-of-school involvement with adolescent "zines." The book concludes with an extensive, thoughtfully compiled annotated bibliography of resources on "gender-fair" literacy learning, computer and visual literacy, gender and schooling, and "boys—the understudied majority."

Barrs, M., & Pidgeon, S. (1998). *Boys and reading.* London: Centre for Language in Primary Education.

> Barrs and Pidgeon began exploring the relationships between reading and gender well before boys' underachievement on standardized assessments of reading began making headlines in the United Kingdom or in the United States. Central to this indispensable volume is the belief that reading is a deeply gendered practice in families, schools, and society as a whole. Barrs' introductory essay follows the evolution of the concern about gender and achievement in reading, outlines various factors that may be contributing to boys' underperformance, and briefly summarizes several responses. The remaining essays provide rare accounts from teachers and researchers of some effective strategies for supporting boys as readers: reading journals (Street and Barrs, Wallace), literature circles (Maclean), reflection to overcome reluctance (Fokias), imaginative play (Pidgeon), and examinations of, and revisions to, the culture of masculinity (Yearwood, Sparkes).

Barrs, M., & Pidgeon, S. (Eds.). (1998). *Reading the difference*. York, ME: Stenhouse.

This collection of essays draws together a variety of voices—those of parents, teachers, researchers, and writers—to describe and reflect upon the emergence of differences in the ways boys and girls learn to read and to think about reading. Although the book as a whole is informed by theory and research, each author speaks in a personal voice and situates his or her observations in a real and recognizable context. The volume includes useful bibliographies of academic studies and children's books.

Crawford, S. H. (1996). *Beyond dolls and guns: 101 ways to help children avoid gender bias*. Portsmouth, NH: Heinemann.

This small book, directed to parents, offers useful bits of "bite-size" advice on how to identify bias in schools and other settings and help children cope with the inequalities they may encounter. The book opens with the often quoted recommendation that to test for sexism one replace gender categories with those of race; although some adults might accept as "normal" that a boy may "hate girls" and refuse to play with them, they would more likely find unacceptable a child's announcement that he "hates blacks" and will not play with them. The book includes a dictionary of nonsexist terminology, sketches of important women in history, and a list of recommended gender-fair children's books.

Davies, B. (1993). *Shards of glass: Children reading and writing beyond gendered identities*. Cresskill, NJ: Hampton Press.

This sequel to *Frogs and Snails and Feminist Tales* (1989) introduces readers to poststructuralist theory in order to analyze how texts "write" or constitute children as their subjects, and how children, in turn, can learn to rewrite and resist dominant texts. Key to Davies' approach is the deconstruction of a set of interlocking and mutually supporting binary divisions that include male/female, mind/body, reason/emotion, independent/connected, and public/private. Davies includes numerous student texts as well as transcripts of interviews and classroom conversations in order to challenge our assumptions about how gender identity is performed and to help us, as well as our students, to read and write "beyond" gendered identities.

Dyson, A. H. (1997). *Writing superheroes: Contemporary childhood, popular culture and classroom literacy*. New York: Teachers College Press.

With a keen eye and ear, and by providing transcripts of children's "Author's Theater" conversation, Dyson invites us into the worlds of Sammy, Tina, and their second grade peers as, over the course of a year, they read, write, speak, and listen their ways to literacy. Dyson examines children's use of popular culture and awareness of diversity to construct identities and to negotiate their place in the social worlds of school and community. In addition to an extensive list of references, the book includes richly detailed media summaries of popular children's films, video games, and television programs.

Dyson, A. H., & Genishi, C. (Eds.). (1994). *The need for story: Cultural diversity in classroom and community.* Urbana, IL: National Council of Teachers of English.

This wide ranging collection includes accessible essays by many leaders in the field of language learning—Maxine Greene, Jerome Bruner, Geneva Smitherman, Vivian Gussin Paley and Shirley Brice Heath—and asks such fundamental questions as "Why do we tell stories? Whose stories are told and heard? How can we build communities through stories?" Although gender is just one facet of diversity addressed in this book, chapters like Bruner's analysis of "Life as Narrative," Gilbert's "And They Lived Happily Ever After" and Paley's "Princess Annabella and the Black Girls" offer memorable readings of student texts that can enhance any teacher's appreciation of the "work" that stories do and the creativity and agency of our youngest students. Even those people most skeptical about the need for gender sensitivity are likely to be compelled by Bruner's conclusion that our stories can "become so habitual that they finally become recipes for structuring experience itself, for laying down routes into memory, for not only guiding the life narrative up to the present, but for directing it into the future" (p. 36).

En-genderings [Special issue]. (2000, March). *Language Arts, 77*(4).

This issue is devoted almost entirely to exploring the ways that literacy learning is tied to how children "learn gender." Among the articles we've found most compelling are Myra Barrs' "Gendered Literacy" (287–293), Thomas Newkirk's "Misreading Masculinity: Speculations on the Great Gender Gap in Writing" (294–300), Heather Blair's "Genderlects: Girl Talk and Boy Talk in a Middle-Years Classroom" (315–323), and Ellen Greever, Patricia Austin, and Karyn Welhousen's "*William's Doll* Revisited" (324–330). A common thread linking these pieces is the call for diversifying literacy practices based on our growing understanding of gender-based strengths and preferences of boys and girls as readers and writers.

Genderizing the curriculum [Special issue]. (1999, January). *English Journal, 88*(3).

"Gender balance" in the English language arts classroom often translates in this themed issue of *English Journal* into combating sexism and encouraging gender equity. Although the primary focus of many of these articles is on honoring the voices of girls and women, there is emerging recognition, within and across the pages of this issue, that teachers must both attend to the differences in the attitudes and abilities of our male and female students and address the topic of gender in and of itself. Especially worth reading are "Gender Roles: Listening to Classroom Talk about Literary Characters," by Barbara Pace and Jane Townsend (43–49); "Mars and Venus in My Classroom: Men Go to Their Caves and Women Talk During Peer Revision," by Mary Styslinger (50–56); "Wimpy Boys and Macho Girls: Gender Equity at the Crossroads," by Lisa McClure (78–82); and "Seeing through the Lenses of Gender: Beyond Male/Female Polarization," by Vicky Greenbaum (96–99). Some of the articles in this issue are suitable for sharing with middle school students and may serve to generate discussion about language, literacy, and gender.

Hicks, D. (2001, January). Literacies and masculinities in the life of a young working-class boy. *Language Arts, 78,* 217–226.

This article exemplifies one of the most powerful lenses through which we may come to understand more about gender and literacy learning—a multi-year study that follows closely the experiences, both at home and in school, of one boy from kindergarten to the early months of third grade. In a manner that is at once sensitive, respectful, and penetrating, Hicks describes Jake's negotiation of gendered identities and literacy learning. Within a family supportive of his development as a reader and writer, Jake develops a set of preferences and expectations from which school-based literacy activities diverge more and more each year. Hicks concludes by admonishing us to make room in the curriculum for textual practices valued by and practiced by boys like Jake.

Kamler, B. (1993, February). Constructing gender in the process writing classroom. *Language Arts, 70,* 20–28.

As part of an ambitious, multi-year study, Kamler follows two children—a boy and a girl—from kindergarten through second grade and analyzes their writing in order to point out subtle but consistent, gendered differences in the ways the two children position themselves, portray events, and describe others. She offers readers useful tools with which to analyze children's writing and concludes that free choice of topic in many process classrooms tacitly encourages children to reproduce culturally defined gender stereotypes.

Millard, E. (1997). *Differently literate: Boys, girls, and the schooling of literacy.* London: Falmer Press.

Situating her year-long study of middle school children's reading and writing choices within her wide-ranging command of the relevant research literature, Millard offers the most ambitious and comprehensive account we have encountered of the ways that boys and girls are "differently literate." In one of the only books to attend to both reading and writing, and to literate behaviors both in and outside of school, Millard offers in-depth explanations of boys' and girl's very different approaches to, and uses of, texts. Millard calls attention to the gendered assumptions that often guide the English Language Arts curriculum and supports her argument for a more inclusive understanding of literacy with dozens of tables and appendices reporting on boys' and girls' favorite books, attitudes toward reading, and topic choices in writing. The book closes with a series of suggestions for pedagogy, many of which have informed the strategies we've recommended here.

Peterson, S. (1998, November). Evaluation and teachers' perception of gender in sixth-grade writing. *Research in the Teaching of English, 33,* 181–208.

Given the predominantly female culture and climate of most elementary and middle school classrooms, it is not surprising that in conversations about assessment, the issue of gender bias often surfaces. One of the few studies we know of to address this issue, and one we strongly recommend, is Peterson's investigation of the relationship between teachers' inferences regarding the author's gender when assessing unidentified writing samples and the impact of those inferences on assigned scores. Peterson determines that the teachers who participated in the study privileged girls' narrative writing, in contrast to the privileging by secondary and postsecondary teachers of male students' persuasive texts.

Pipher, M. (1994). *Reviving Ophelia: Saving the selves of adolescent girls*. New York: Putnam.

Clinical psychologist Mary Pipher uses case studies and an engaging, often dramatic style to paint a disturbing portrait of contemporary female adolescence. Highlighting the ways that American culture establishes unattainable and damaging ideas of female beauty and erodes young women's self-esteem, Pipher concludes that our "girl-poisoning" society forces a choice on girls between being shunned for staying true to a sense of self and struggling to stay within a narrow definition of the ideal female. The book includes strategies for helping girls resist social pressures and develop a strong and individual sense of self.

Pollack, W. (1998). *Real boys: Rescuing our sons from the myths of boyhood*. New York: Henry Holt & Co.

Like Myriam Miedzian's *Boys Will Be Boys* (New York: Anchor Books, 1991) that preceded it and much like Kindlon and Thompson's *Raising Cain: Protecting the Emotional Life of Boys* (New York: Ballantine, 1999) that followed, *Real Boys* argues that just as Betty Friedan revealed a "feminine mystique that succeeded in burying millions of American women alive," so in the 1990s a "masculine mystique" or "boy code" continues to create unrealistic expectations that harm boys and men and prevent their healthy flourishing. Directed primarily to parents, the book uses numerous case studies to reveal the "myths of boyhood" and to suggest effective interventions through which parents and educators can challenge these myths, work with boys in order to read their moods and emotions, and help boys become confident, empathic and empowered men with genuine voices of their own.

Sadker, M., & Sadker, D. (1994). *Failing at fairness: How America's schools cheat girls*. New York: Charles Scribner's Sons.

In this comprehensive and compelling volume, the Sadkers reveal what they call the "hidden lessons" of inequality and sexism that students learn at all levels of schooling from preschool to doctoral programs. Drawing on an extensive body of published research as well as their own carefully documented classroom observations, the book makes visible the pervasive, and therefore seemingly "normal," classroom and curricular practices that silence girls, erode their self-esteem and create a "chilly climate" for learning. In response to readers' many requests, the book contains an extensive recommended reading list of children's books with strong female characters at their center. You may be surprised to learn that the book also includes a prophetic chapter on the "miseducation of boys" that anticipates many recent discussions of the ways that boys are also disadvantaged and damaged by gender stereotyping.

Tannen, D. (1990). *You just don't understand: Women and men in conversation.* New York: Ballantine.

Despite its status as the informal "pop-psych" best-seller that inspired dozens of jokes about asking for directions, Tannen's book provides a theoretically rich framework through which to understand many differences in male and female communication styles. Tannen's claim that in communication women are more likely to seek connection and attend to the "metamessage" whereas men are more likely to engage in competition and to attend to the informational content, is substantiated by countless other studies and helps to explain many of the differences we and other researchers have noticed in boys' and girls' writing. Tannen alerts her readers that, much as in this book we speak of what boys and girls "tend to" do, she also generalizes across race and region, preparing the ground for future work.

Thomas, P. (1997). Doom to the red-eyed nyungghns from the planet glarg: Boys as writers of narrative. *English in Education, 31*(3), 23–31.

Starting from the premise that boys and girls are differently literate, Thomas argues that the best route to increased competence on the part of both is to identify and work with their respective strengths. Using driving as an extended metaphor for the narrative journey, Thomas is as engaging and effective in describing boys' stories as anyone we know; what especially resonated for us were such observations as, "With boy's, it's all maximum revs. Each action incident is another gear change and acceleration" (24) and "[Boys] need more negotiating and navigating skills and less assertive use of the accelerator (or exhilarator!)" (25). Thomas does an excellent job of describing and defining the strengths of both boys and girls as writers and suggests that rather than favoring one over the other, we encourage a mix of both "command and control" and "care and respond" tendencies in all young writers regardless of their gender.

Wilhelm, J. (1997). *"You gotta BE the book": Teaching engaged and reflective reading with adolescents.* New York: Teachers College Press.

Wilhelm observes the reading habits and strategies of his most engaged middle school readers in order to develop both an expanded theory of reading response, and with it, a pedagogy that has the power to involve his most reluctant readers. Believing that students must be fully engaged—must "be" the book—before they can respond critically to texts, Wilhelm describes a series of arts-based activities from visualizations to dramatizations in order to fully involve reluctant readers in fictional worlds. The book contains useful appendices that outline lesson plans and list questions and activities to support the ten distinct dimensions of reader response that Wilhelm analyzes.

# CHILDREN'S LITERATURE CITED

Adler, David. (1997). *Cam Jansen and the Mystery of the Dinosaur Bones*. Illustrated by Susanna Natti. New York: Puffin.

Adler, David. (1997). *Cam Jansen and the Mystery of the Stolen Diamonds*. Illustrated by Susanna Natti. New York: Puffin.

Adler, David. (1997). *Cam Jansen and the Mystery of the UFO*. Illustrated by Susanna Natti. New York: Puffin.

Alexander, Lloyd. (1990). *The El Dorado Adventure*. New York: Bantam Doubleday.

Alexander, Lloyd. (1990). *The Illyrian Adventure*. New York: Bantam Doubleday.

Alexander, Lloyd. (1999). *The Jedera Adventure*. Minneapolis: Econo-Clad Books.

Alexander, Lloyd. (1999). *The Philadelphia Adventure*. Minneapolis: Econo-Clad Books.

Alexander, Lloyd. (2001). *The Drackenberg Adventure*. New York: Puffin.

Allaby, Michael. (1999). *How the Weather Works*. New York: Readers Digest.

Amjera, Maya, & Versola, Ama. (1997). *Children from Australia to Zimbabwe*. Watertown: Charlesbridge Publishing.

Avi. (1992). *True Confessions of Charlotte Doyle*. Illustrated by Ruth E. Murray. New York: Avon Books.

Cannon, Janell. (1994). *Stella Luna*. New York: Scholastic Books.

Carbone, Elisa. (2001). *Storm Warriors*. New York: Knopf.

Carlson, Laurie. (1998). *Days of Knights and Damsels: An Activity Guide*. Chicago: Chicago Review Press.

Child, Lauren. (2000). *I Will Never Not Eat a Tomato*. Cambridge, MA: Candlewick Press.

Cohen, Daniel. (1998). *Dinosaur Discovery: Facts, Fossils and Fun*. Illustrated by Russel Farrell. New York: Puffin

Cooney, Barbara. (1985). *Miss Rumphius*. New York: Viking Press.

Corey, Shana. (1999). *You Forgot Your Skirt, Amelia Bloomer.* Illustrated by Chelsea Mc-Laren. New York: Scholastic.

Crutcher, Chris. *Staying Fat for Sarah Barnes.* (Also, *Stotan!, Athletic Shorts, Running Loose.*) New York: Laurel Leaf.

Curtis, Christopher Paul. (1997). *The Watsons Go to Birmingham—1963*. New York: Bantam.

Cushman, Karen. (1995). *Catherine, Called Bird*. New York: Harper Trophy.

Cushman, Karen. (1996). *The Midwife's Apprentice*. New York: Harper Trophy.

Cushman, Karen. (1998). *The Ballad of Lucy Whipple*. New York: HarperCollins Juvenile Books.

Cushman, Karen. (2000). *Matilda Bone*. Lander: Clarion Books.

Dahl. Roald. (1995). *Roald Dahl's Revolting Rhymes*. Illustrated by Quentin Blake. New York: Puffin.

Dalgliesh, Alice (1991). *The Courage of Sarah Noble*. Illustrated by Leonard Weisgard. New York: Simon and Schuster.

De Angeli, Marguerite. *A Door in the Wall*. (1990). New York: Dell.

De Paola, Tomie. (1990). *Oliver Button is a Sissy*. New York: Harcourt Brace.

Disalvo-Ryan, Dyanne, & Reisberg, Mira (1997). *Uncle Willie and the Soup Kitchen*. Keighly: Mulberry Books.

Ellis, Deborah. (2000). *The Breadwinner*. Toronto: Groundwood Books.

Ernst, Lisa Campbell. (1992). *Sam Johnson and the Blue Ribbon Quilt*. Keighly: Mulberry Books.

Ernst, Lisa Campbell. (2000). *Goldilocks Returns*. New York: Simon & Schuster Children's.

Fitzhugh, Louise (2001). *Harriet the Spy*. New York: Yearling Books.

Fleischman, Paul.(1996). *Dateline Troy*. Illustrated by Gwen Frankfeldt. New York: Candlewick Press.

Fleischman, Paul. (1998). *Joyful Noise: Poems for Two Voices*. Illustrated by Eric Beddows. New York: HarperCollins Juvenile Books.

Florian, Douglas. (1998). *Beast Feast*. New York: Voyager Picture Book.

Florian, Douglas. (1998). *Insectlopedia*. New York: Harcourt Brace.

Ford, Juwanda. (1996). *A Kente Dress for Kenya*. Illustrated by Sylvia Walker. New York: Cartwheel Books.

Gray, Nigel. (1998). *A Country Far Away*. Illustrated by Philippe Dupasquier. New York: Orchard Books.

Honan, Linda. (1998). *Spend the Day in Ancient Greece*. Illustrated by Ellen Kosmer. New York: John Wiley and Sons.

Huck, Charlotte. (1994). *Princess Furball*. Illustrated by Anita Lobel. Keighley: Mulberry Books

Hughes, Dean. (1999). *Play Ball (Scrappers, No. 1)*. New York: Aladdin Paperback.

Juster, Norton. (1993). *The Phantom Tollbooth*. Illustrated by Jules Fieffer. New York: Random House.

Kindersley, Anabel, & Kindersley, Barnabas. (1995). *Children Just Like Me*. London: Dorling Kindersley Ltd.

King, David. (1999). *Civil War Days*. New York: John Wiley and Sons.

*Knights & Castles*. (1995). New York: Kids Discover Magazine.

Levine, Gail Carson. (1997). *Ella Enchanted*. New York: Harper Trophy.

Levine, Gail Carson. (2001). *The Two Princesses of Bammare*. New York: HarperColins.

Lowell, Susan. (1992). *Three Javelinas*. Illustrated by Jim Harris. Rising Moon Press.

Masini, Beatrice, and Handley, Diana. (2000) *A Brave Little Princess*. Illustrated by Octavia Monaco. Cambridge, MA: Barefoot Books.

Mazer, Anne. (1994). *The Salamander Room*. Illustrated by Lou Fancher and Steve Johnson. New York: Knopf.

McDonald, Megan.(1997). *Insects Are My Life*. Illustrated by Paul Brett Johnson. New York: Orchard Books.

McGovern, Ann. (1992). *If You Lived in Colonial Times*. Illustrated by June Otani and Brinton Turkle. New York: Scholastic Trade.

Merill, Jean. (1997). *The Girl Who Loved Caterpillars: A Twelfth Century Tale from Japan*. Illustrated by Floyd Cooper. New York: Paper Star.

Minters, Frances. (1997). *Cinder-Elly*. Illustrated by Brian Karas. New York: Puffin.

Moss, Jeffrey. (1997). *Bone Poems*. New York: Workman Publishing Company.

Munsch, Robert N. (1998). *Paper Bag Princess*. Illustrated by Michael Martchenko. Toronto: Annick Press.

Murphy, Jim. (1992). *The Long Road to Gettysburg*. Lander: Clarion Books.

Onyefulu, Ifeoma. (1999). *Ebele's Favorite: A Book of African Games*. London: Frances Lincoln.

Peirce, Tamora (1989). *Allana: The First Adventure*. New York: Random House.

Peirce, Tamora. (1998). *In the Hand of the Goddess*. New York: Random House.

Peirce, Tamora. (1998). *Lioness Rampant*. New York: Random House.

Powell, Anton, & Steele, Philip. (1999). *The Greek News*. Cambridge, MA: Candlewick Press.

Prelutsky, Jack (1984) *The New Kid on the Block*. Illustrated by James Stevenson. New York: Greenwillow.

Prelutsky, Jack. (1990). *Something Big Has Been Here*. Illustrated by James Stevenson. New York: William Morrow and Company.

Prelutsky, Jack. (1996). *A Pizza the Size of the Sun*. Illustrated by James Stevenson. New York: Greenwillow.

Pullman, Phillip. (1996). *The Golden Compass*. New York: Knopf.

Pullman, Phillip. (1999). *The Subtle Knife*. New York: Del Rey.

Pullman, Phillip. (2000). *The Amber Spyglass*. New York: Knopf.

Rennert, Richard. (1994). *Profiles of Great Black Americans: Female Leaders*. New York: Chelsea House Publishers.

Rinaldi, Ann. (2001). *Girl in Blue*. New York: Scholastic.

Robertson Jr., James I. (1992). *Civil War: America Becomes One Nation*. New York: Knopf.

Ross, Kathy. (1997). *Crafts for Kids Who are Wild About Dinosaurs*; entire *Crafts for Kids* series. New York: Millbrook Press Trade.

Rowling, R. K. *Harry Potter* (series). New York: Scholastic.

Sachar, Louis. (1999). *Holes*. New York: Yearling.

San Souci, Robert D. (1998). *A Weave of Words: An Armenian Tale*. Illustrated by Raul Colon. New York: Orchard Books.

Scieszka, Jon. (1991). *The True Story of the Three Little Pigs*. Illustrated by Lane Smith. Minneapolis: Econoclad Books.

Sexton, Anne. (1998). *Transformations*. New York: Mariner Books.

Sneddon, Robert. (1994). *What is an Amphibian?* Illustrated by Adrian Lascom. Boston: Little Brown.

Snicket, Lemony. (1999, 2000, 2001). *A Series of Unfortunate Events (Books 1-6)*. New York: HarperCollins.

Speigelman, Art. (1973, 1986). *Maus I and II*. New York: Pantheon Books.

Spinelli, Jerry. (1999). *Wringer*. New York: Harper Trophy.

Suzuki, David. (1992). *Looking at Insects*. New York: John Wiley & Sons.

Taylor, Theodore. (1991). *The Cay*. New York: Avon.

Thompson, Lauren. (2001). *One Riddle, One Answer*. New York: Scholastic.

Trivizas, Eugene. (1992). *Three Little Wolves and the Big Bad Pig*. Illustrated by Helen Oxenbury. New York: Alladin Books.

Turck, Mary. (2000). *The Civil Rights Movement for Kids: A History with 21 Activities*. Chicago: Chicago Review Press.

VanCleave, Janice. (1991). *Earth Science for Every Kid: 101 Experiments that Really Work*. New York: John Wiley & Sons.

Williams, V. B. (1984). *Three Days on a River In a Red Canoe*. New York: Greenwillow.

Winter, Kathryn. (1998). *Katarina*. New York: Scholastic Signature.

Winthrop, Elizabeth. (2001). *Dumpy La Rue*. Illustrated by Betsey Lewen. New York: Henry Holt and Company.

Yolen, Jane. (1988). *The Devil's Arithmetic*. New York: Puffin.

# REFERENCES

A Very Harry Halloween. (2000, October 27) [World report ed.]. *Time for Kids 6* (7), 8.

AAUW. (1992). *How schools shortchange girls.* Washington, DC: AAUW.

Adler, S. (1994). Great adventures and everyday events. In M. Barrs & S. Pidgeon (Eds.), *Reading the difference* (pp. 81–87). York, ME: Stenhouse.

Atwell, N. (1998). *In the middle: New understandings about writing, reading, and learning.* Portsmouth, NH: Boynton/Cook.

Atwood, M. (1978). The curse of Eve: Or what I learned in school. In A. Shteir (Ed.), *Women on women* (pp. 13–26). Toronto: York UP.

Barrs, M. (2000, March). Gendered literacy? *Language Arts, 77*(4), 287–293.

Barrs, M., & Pidgeon, S. (1998). *Boys and reading.* London: Centre for Language in Primary Education.

Barrs, M., & Pidgeon, S., (Eds.). (1998). *Reading the difference.* York, ME: Stenhouse.

Bowman, C. A. (1992). Gender differences in response to literature. In N. M. McCracken & B. C. Appleby (Eds.), *Gender issues in the teaching of English* (pp. 80–92). Urbana, IL: National Council of Teachers of English.

Brownstein, R. (1982). *Becoming a heroine.* Harmondsworth, England: Penguin.

Calkins, L. M. (1994). *The art of teaching writing.* Portsmouth, NH: Heinemann.

Calkins, L. M. (2000). *The art of teaching reading.* New York: Longman.

Crawford, M. (1995). *Talking difference: On gender and language.* London: Sage Publications.

Davies, B. (1989). *Frogs and snails and feminist tales: Preschool children and gender.* Sydney: Allen & Unwin.

Davies, B. (1993). *Shards of glass: Children reading and writing beyond gendered identities.* Cresskill, NJ: Hampton Press.

Davies, J., & Brember, I. (1993). Comics or stories?: Differences in the reading attitudes and habits of girls and boys in years 2, 4 and 6. *Gender and Education, 5*(3), 305–320.

Dyson, A. H. (1997). *Writing superheroes: Contemporary childhood, popular culture and classroom literacy.* New York: Teachers College Press.

En-genderings [Special issue]. (2000, March). *Language Arts 77*(4).

Epstein, D., Elwood, H., Hey, V., & Maw, J. (1998). *Failing boys? Issues in gender and achievement.* Philadelphia, PA: Open University Press.

Fetterley, J. (1978*). The resisting reader: A feminist approach to American fiction.* Bloomington, IN: Indiana University Press.

Freedman, R. A. (1995). The Mr. and Mrs. club: The value of collaboration in writers' workshop. *Language Arts, 72,* 97–104.

Frye, M. (1983). *The politics of reality.* Freedom, CA: Crossing Press.

Garber, M. (2001, April 8). The chapter after 'the end.' *The New York Times,* section 4, p. 15.

Gilbert, P. (1994). "And they lived happily ever after": Cultural storylines and the construction of gender. In A. H. Dyson & C. Genishi (Eds.), *The Need for Story.* Urbana, IL: National Council of Teachers of English.

Gilligan, C. (1982*). In a different voice: Psychological theory and women's development.* Cambridge, MA: Harvard University Press.

Hammerberg, D. D. (2001, January). Reading and writing "hypertextually": Children's literature, technology, and early writing instruction. *Language Arts 78*(3), 207–216.

Harvey, S. (2000). *Nonfiction matters.* Portland, ME: Stenhouse.

Hicks, D. (2001, January). Literacies and masculinities in the life of a young working-class boy. *Language Arts 78*(3), 217–226.

Hilton, M. (Ed.). (1996). *Potent fictions: Children's literacy and the challenge of popular culture.* New York: Routledge.

Hourihan, M. (1997*). Deconstructing the hero: Literary theory and children's literature.* London and New York: Routledge.

Hynes, M. (2000, July). "I read for facts": Reading nonfiction in a fictional world." *Language Arts, 77*(6), 485–495.

Kamler, B. (1993, February). Constructing gender in the writing process classroom. *Language Arts, 70,* 95–103.

Kentucky Department of Education. (2000). Minimum student achievement performance data. Frankfort, KY: KDE.

Kerper, R. M., Aoki, E., and Duthie, C. (2000, November). Outstanding nonfiction choices for 1999. *Language Arts 78*(2), 177–184.

Kindlon, D., & Thompson, M. (1999). *Raising Cain: Protecting the emotional life of boys.* New York: Ballantine.

Lane, B. (1993). *After the end: Teaching and learning creative revision.* Portsmouth, NH: Heinemann.

Langer, J. A. (1989). *The process of understanding literature.* (Report Series 2.1). Albany, NY: Center for Learning and Teaching of Literature.

Langer, J. A. (1990, October). The process of understanding: Reading for literary and informative purposes. *Research in the Teaching of English, 24*(3), 229–260.

Matthews, M. W., & Kesner, J. E. (2000, February). The silencing of Sammy: One struggling reader learning with his peers. *The Reading Teacher 53*(5), 382–390.

McCracken, N. M., & Appleby, B. C. (1992). *Gender issues in the teaching of English.* Urbana, IL: National Council of Teachers of English.

McMillon, G. T. & Edwards, P. A. (2000, November). Why does Joshua "hate" school… but love Sunday school? *Language Arts 78*(2), 111–120.

Maryland State Department of Education. (2000). *2000 Maryland School Performance Report.* Baltimore, MD: MSDE.

Millard, E. (1997). *Differently literate: Boys, girls, and the schooling of literacy.* London: Falmer Press.

Moss, B., Leone, S., & Dipillo, M. L. (1997, October). Exploring the literature of fact: Linking reading and writing through information trade books. *Language Arts, 74*(6): 418–429.

*NAEP 1998 Reading Report Card for the Nation and the States.* (1998). Washington, DC: National Assessment of Educational Progress.

National Assessment Governing Board (1992). *Reading framework for the 1992 National Assessment of Educational Progress.* Authors.

Newkirk, T. (2000, March). Misreading masculinity: Speculations on the great gender gap in writing. *Language Arts, 77*(4), 294–300.

OSPI (Office of Superintendent of Public Instruction). Education Profile [On-line]. Olympia: Washington State Department of Education. Available: http://www.k12.wa.us/EdProfile.

OFSTED (Office for Standards in Education). (1993). *Boys and English.* (Ref. 2/ 93/ NS). London: Department for Education.

OFSTED/EOC (Office for Standards in Education and Equal Opportunities Commission). (1996). *The gender divide: Performance differences between boys and girls at school.* London: HMSO.

Orenstein, P. (1994*). Schoolgirls: Young women, self-esteem, and the confidence gap.* New York: Doubleday.

Paley, V. (1984). *Boys & girls: Superheroes in the doll corner.* Chicago: University of Chicago Press.

Peterson, S. (1998, November). Evaluation and teachers' perception of gender in sixth-grade student writing. *Research in the Teaching of English, 33,* 181–208.

Peterson, S. (2001, May). Gender identities and self-expression in classroom narrative writing. *Language Arts 78*(5), 451–457.

Pipher, M. (1994). *Reviving Ophelia: Saving the selves of adolescent girls.* New York: Ballantine Books.

Pollack, W. (1998). *Real boys: Rescuing our sons from the myths of boyhood.* New York: Henry Holt & Co.

Portalupi, J., & Fletcher, R. (2001). *Nonfiction craft lessons: Teaching information writing K-8.* Portland, ME: Stenhouse.

Power, B. & Hubbard, R. (1999, September). Becoming teacher researchers one moment at a time. *Language Arts 77*(1), 34–39.

Rosenblatt, L. (1978). *The reader, the text, the poem: The transactional theory of literary work.* Carbondale, IL: Southern Illinois UP.

Sadker, M., & Sadker, D. (1994). *Failing at fairness: How America's schools cheat girls.* New York: Scribners.

Schneider, J. J. (2001, May). No blood, guns or gays allowed!: The silencing of the elementary writer. *Language Arts 78*(5), 415–425.

Simmons, J. (1997, February). Attack of the killer baby faces: Gender similarities in third grade writing. *Language Arts, 74*(3), 116–123.

Sommers, C.H. (2001). *The war against boys.* New York: Touchstone Books.

Sullivan, E. (2001, January). Some teens prefer the real thing: The case for young adult non-fiction. *English Journal 90*(3), 43–47.

Tannen, D. (1990). *You just don't understand: Women and men in conversation.* New York: Ballantine.

Thomas, P. (1997). Doom to the red-eyed nyungghns from the planet glarg: Boys as writers of narrative. *English in Education, 31*(3), 23–31.

The truth about nonfiction [Call for manuscripts]. (2000, March). *English Journal 90*(4), 9.

Vermont Department of Education. (2000). Are there gender differences in performance [On-line]? *School Improvement Support Guide.* Available: http://data.ed.state.vt.us/apg/q4graph.asp.

Wilhelm, J. (1997). *"You gotta BE the book": Teaching engaged and reflective reading with adolescents.* New York: Teachers College Press.

Worthy, J., Moorman, M., & Turner, M. (1999). What Johnny likes to read is hard to find in school. *Reading Research Quarterly 34*(1), 12–27.